MW00574390

HAUNTED
OCEAN CITY
AND BERLIN

HAUNTED OCEAN CITY AND BERLIN

MINDIE BURGOYNE

Foreword by Helen Chappell

Haunted
America

Published by Haunted America
A Division of The History Press
Charleston, SC 29403
www.historypress.net

Cover image: Photograph of the Ocean City Life-Saving Station. *Courtesy of Jim Lamm.*
Opposite: The Trimper Menagerie Carousel.

First published 2014

ISBN 978-1-5402-1211-5

Library of Congress CIP data applied for.

To Sweet Pea and Sweet Tater...

Twins of my heart who traveled with me as I researched this book and allowed me to see the ghosts of Ocean City and Berlin through a child's eyes.

CONTENTS

CONTENTS

FOREWORD

Welcome to haunted Ocean City and Berlin.

What you hold in your hands is not your average beach read—a quick and easy way to while away a sunny afternoon in the sand or a rainy day stuck inside. No, this is much more fun. And much more chilling because these tales of the old days really did happen—and might still be happening even as you read this.

The land between the ocean and the Bay has a long, ancient history beneath the creosote boardwalks, the concrete abutments and the candy-colored condos. A great deal of this history isn't dead. It's not even passed. If you glance out of the side of your eye, you might see just the edge of an old-fashioned petticoat or a sinister-looking sea captain. But they're not really there, are they? That step on the stairs, that faint burst of childish laughter—was that a distant scream in the night?

Or is it something, well, ghostly?

So you thought the beach was all cotton candy, salt water taffy and promenading on the Boardwalk? You believed that the small town of Berlin was a peaceful old hamlet where nothing ever happened or ever will? That these staid old resort towns where Chesapeake Bay meets the Atlantic Ocean would never entertain restless spirits or unhappy endings? Bwahaha. Prepare to have your spine tingle on this tour through the supernatural.

Welcome to Mindie Burgoyne's world, where nothing is as it seems and the unknown and undead linger in the most unlikely places. Think Trimper's landmark amusement park on the boards is all bright lights and great rides? Behind the tinsel and twinkle, a ghost is flickering between the bumper cars and the carousel.

Those footsteps on the Boardwalk? Don't turn around. There may not be a living person behind you. At the historic Atlantic Hotel, one of the original resorts of Ocean City, built by the Lower Shore Purnell family, people have checked in and never checked out.

The Atlantic has a long history, and in the place where the ocean meets the dunes, haunts and happenings abound. The drowned, the shipwrecked, the lovelorn and the beloved all have their stories here. And if you're lucky, you might see, or hear or…feel them. Is that the laughter of children you hear? Are they children in the here and now or children from long ago, still lingering? Is that tree haunted or is it just the wind?

Come meet the spirits of innkeepers, jazz singers, writers, watermen and seafood packers and the restless ghost of one Charles Rackliffe, a cruel master who was murdered by his slaves and still wanders his old property, looking for revenge and a way to make you very, very uncomfortable.

Farther inland, there's another Atlantic Hotel in Berlin, where Horace Harmonson opened the red brick landmark, where the spirits of old traveling salesmen still roam the halls, doubtless looking for a different kind of spirits altogether.

Come visit with ghosts and elementals, jilted lovers and lost lifeguards in eighteen tales told only as Mindie Burgoyne can, guaranteed to freeze your blood and make you look behind you on a moonlit night on the beach.

HELEN CHAPPELL
Trappe, Maryland, 2014
Author of *The Oysterback Tales* and *Chesapeake Book of the Dead*

ACKNOWLEDGEMENTS

Haunted Ocean City and Berlin grew out of the ghost walks I crafted for these two towns. Gathering the information for those walks was the foundation for the content in this book. There were several key people who helped me dig into the history, find the ghost stories, verify facts, locate photographs and find sources for interviews. Without their assistance, I'd never have been able to craft the walks or write this book.

My deepest thanks go to Glenn Irwin, executive director of the Ocean City Development Corporation, who set aside an hour during the workweek to meet with me, map out the historic part of the town and give me the names of key people who could help me with the stories and information I needed to put a ghost walk together. Glenn opened all the right doors for me and helped make the process swift. From historians to artists to town officials, Glenn knew who would help me. And they did.

I'd also like to thank the Ocean City Life-Saving Station Museum. The museum's executive director, Sandy Hurley, and her staff helped me navigate this vast repository of the town's history. Sandy in particular was able to answer so many of my questions when I found gaps in the history or confusion over dates or family names. She is such an asset to Worcester County, as is that amazing museum.

I sincerely appreciate the cooperation I received from the business owners in Ocean City whose properties are featured in this book. Charlie Purnell and Denise from the Atlantic Hotel, Greg Shockley from the Shoreham Hotel and Anna Dolle-Bushnell from Dolle's Candyland were all generous with their time, stories and support. A special word of thanks goes to Brooks Trimper and Johnny Jett from Trimper's Amusements who provided me with a magical, romantic tale that has become my favorite ghost story.

I conducted many personal interviews during my research. One of the most valuable resources for the Ocean City portion of this book was my interview with Ocean City historians George and Sue Hurley. I so appreciate them welcoming me, with my nine-year-old granddaughter in tow, into their home for an interview. These two have so many Ocean City memories and stories between them. I feel lucky for the time we shared. I'd also like to thank Betty Jester and Richard Manse for recounting their story of the little boy they saw in the Life-Saving Station Museum, Jo Ellen West for her memories of the Tarry-A-While and Denise Milko and Missy Mason for their insights on Rackliffe House.

In Berlin, my greatest ally has been Angela Reynolds, general manager of the Atlantic Hotel. Angela has given up her time to share stories about the hotel, been supportive of our ghost walk efforts and partnered with us to promote Berlin's haunted heritage. I also appreciate the cooperation and assistance of the Calvin B. Taylor House Museum, especially Cheryl Holland and Susan Taylor, and the guys at Adkins Hardware who shared their stories.

Author and attorney Joe Moore gave me a one-hour interview that included a concise history of Berlin, its heroes and its crazy characters. There was enough in that interview to intrigue any writer, and his stories are so rich with detail. Joe is as entertaining as he is informative, and he is a gifted storyteller. Snippets of his stories are woven into most of the Berlin tales in this book. Special thanks also to Kirk Burbage, who cleared up the mystery of why no people are buried in Ocean City.

As with everything I write about Maryland's history, I gratefully acknowledge the Edward H. Nabb Research Center at Salisbury University and its Folklore Collection. Several pieces of folklore from the Nabb are included in stories in this book and are so noted. Also, thank you to the Worcester County Library, the Maryland Historical Trust, Anna Dolle Bushnell, the Dunes Manor Hotel and the Atlantic Hotel for giving me access to photographs used in this book. Credit is noted in the captions for specific photographs. If no credit is noted in the caption, the images were either photographed by me or are from my postcard collection.

I also offer special thanks to the folks at The History Press, especially Hannah Cassilly, Magan Thomas and Brittain Phillips. They've been so attentive to my requests and always willing to work with me. The History

Press makes it easy for authors to get their books into the hands of the general public. I'm happy to have another book published by this company.

Finally, I thank the one person who makes my writing possible. My husband, Dan Burgoyne, is there when I need him and there when I don't know that I need him. He cooks; he cleans; he takes care of the house, the animals and the cars; and he manages our ghost walk business. When I'm furiously writing, he delivers meals to my desk. This also includes coffee in the morning and wine in the evening and an occasional flower from our garden. Dan is my stronghold, my support, my friend, my lover and my soul mate. Every word I type has his support behind it in some small way. And because he is in my life, I feel compelled to write.

Introduction

When Isaac Coffin erected the first cottage that housed overnight guests in 1869, the area now known as Ocean City wasn't much more than a sand dune. His lodgers were mostly hunters and fishermen from the Lower Eastern Shore, and the barrier island stretched from the Indian River Inlet in Delaware all the way down to Virginia, where Tom's Cove joins the Chincoteague Inlet. Small fishing camps and rooming houses sprang up over the next few years, but the barrier island still had almost no population.

In 1874, a group of investors met in Salisbury and devised a plan to build a resort hotel not too far from Coffin's guest house. They decided to name the town Ocean City, and in less than a year, construction began on the Atlantic Hotel. It was built in the Victorian style and occupied an entire city block. Rather than appealing to semi-local hunters and fishermen, it was built to attract the financial elite from the big cities like Baltimore, New York and Philadelphia. It opened on July 4, 1875. That is when Ocean City was born.

What makes Ocean City so interesting—and so different from most small towns on the Eastern Shore—is that it was never really a hometown. All the towns that grew up along the Delmarva waterways developed around some sort of manufacturing or trade. A town may have started as a trading post for beaver pelts and tobacco and then developed into shipbuilding or seafood distribution. But almost all the towns grew as a result of a particular manufacturing industry or being a hub of trade. As those businesses grew around that trade, more people came to settle in

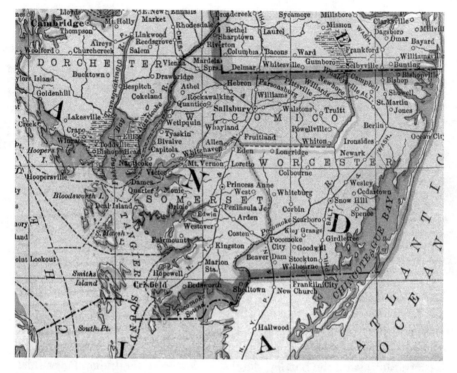

Hammond's map of Maryland and Delaware, 1908. *Image courtesy of the Nabb Research Center, Salisbury University.*

the town and more support services were added. Clusters of trade grew into villages. Villages grew into towns. Some towns grew into cities, and families put down roots that eventually spanned many generations. But Ocean City didn't follow this model.

Ocean City was created for tourists who came in the summer and left when the season was over. It never had another purpose other than to serve tourists. Today, almost 140 years later, with a population that has swelled to seven thousand permanent residents, Ocean City locals still feel that stark contrast between winter and summer. The town hibernates all winter; then comes spring, and with spring comes the transformation, the anticipation and that not-so-subtle surge of excitement just before the crowds descend. The hearts of the vacationers beat a little faster as they anticipate a visit to the seaside—the seaside town to which they always return: Ocean City.

This is what makes Ocean City's haunted history so endearing. It seems that almost all of the ghosts in these stories want to return to where they spent their best times, to where they were woven into the fabric of the town's mystique. Ocean City has happy ghosts. And when you get out and walk the streets, you can conjure up the one-hundred-year-old pulse of that seaside town.

From the Inlet all the way to 28th Street, where the Boardwalk ends, you can imagine the ladies in their long white summer dresses and the men in their seersucker suits. You can feel distant vibrations in the old wooden structures connecting you to that time long ago.

You can sense the presence of Rudolph Dolle as you taste some salt water taffy. You might catch the scent of Joanne Trimper's perfume as you ride Trimper's Menagerie Carousel. The old spirits are still moving in and out of the landscape, and the sensitive visitor notices. Perhaps you'll feel the warm welcome of Thelma Connors serving tea at the Dunes Manor, or notice Dr. Charles Purnell and his wife, Flossie, greeting guests that step off the train at the Atlantic Hotel, or catch a glimpse of Zippy Lewis in the early morning mist searching for coins on the beach or hear Louis Armstrong and Cab Calloway jamming at the Henry Hotel.

Those spirits remain in Ocean City because the happiness never ends. It's a continuous cycle of hopeful tourists spending the best times of their lives. All the memories of this place that are scattered over time are connected. Each one energizes the next. It's through this web of memories that the spirits of Ocean City reach out to us.

There's never been such a happy haunted town. Well, there are a few not-so-happy ghosts—like the guy who was murdered at the Shoreham Hotel and the young man who despaired so badly over a lost love that he took his own life. But they're in the minority.

Like Ocean City, Berlin also entertained tourists. It was incorporated shortly after the Civil War and was an attractive area for sportsmen who loved hunting and fishing. It was also a stopping place for those on their way to the Atlantic beaches in Ocean City a mere nine miles away. What most people don't know is that Berlin was also a stopping place for salesmen who would market products to store merchants and tradesmen. They were called "drummers" because they were drumming up business. The Atlantic Hotel in Berlin provided overnight accommodations for these drummers, which was the impetus for naming the hotel's excellent restaurant the Drummer's Café.

There is nothing quite like that Atlantic Hotel. Not to be confused with the Atlantic Hotel that started Ocean City, this Atlantic Hotel dominates the Berlin streetscape like a bride dominates a wedding. It is the star of the town; it is the anchor of the main street. Every other building and fixture serves as an ornament and stands in its grand shadow. The Atlantic Hotel has a character all its own that speaks a welcome in the daytime and gives a peaceful benediction in the evening, when guests can watch the day fade away from big porch rockers in the courtyard. Visitors and locals alike never tire of gazing on this Victorian wonder or standing in its regal presence. And perhaps this is why the spirits won't leave. The spirits of the Atlantic Hotel—a child, a family, a woman who needs towels, a phantom guest who snags wrapped gifts and then returns them, a drummer who swipes tools from maintenance men—all are friendly and very much at home. They don't want to leave.

The architecture and streetscapes are so intact that Berlin has become the poster child for having that "old town" feel and has attracted Hollywood producers to use Berlin's streets as a setting for their movies. Both *The Runaway Bride* in 1999, distributed by Paramount Pictures, and *Tuck Everlasting* in 2002, distributed by Buena Vista Pictures, were filmed in Berlin. Unlike the Eastern Shore towns that grew up around a waterway, Berlin grew up around a railroad. The railroad opened up opportunities for travel that the world had never seen. And in Berlin, two rail lines crossed, making it a popular jumping-off point.

Jobs in agriculture employed the greatest number of local people in Berlin one hundred years ago, and this was largely due to the success of Senator Orlando Harrison and the Harrison Brothers Nurseries, which employed between 250 and 500 people depending on the season. The agriculture, retail trade and tourism industries that flourished in this railroad town spun off many shoulder or support businesses and generated an elite wealthy class in Berlin that occupied some of the most beautiful Victorian-style homes on the Eastern Shore.

Berlin was a town of merchants, politicians, bankers and crazy characters. And the spirits of some of those characters are still hanging around. The ghost of Ned France, a magician and junk shop dealer who once dressed in chains and hung himself upside down from a store awning, is still seen walking down the vacant main street after midnight. Noise from partiers at the old speakeasy are still heard by one commercial building occupant, and the Adkins Hardware store has two known ghosts and an elemental creature that has been photographed numerous times. Spirits of general store owners, bankers, botanists and soldiers have all interacted with residents of Berlin.

When a storyteller weaves a haunted tale about ghosts peeping through the veil that separates this world from the spirit world, the listener inevitably questions why the ghost is there. Why do spirits haunt places?

Language fails us when we try to explain such things. And sometimes it never makes sense.

The rationalist will say hauntings can't be real because they can't be proven. Paranormal experts will figure things out based on scientific principles and throw out what they can't explain. But most ordinary people just wonder. And buried in that sense of wonder is where we find the answers about the spirits that haunt us. The little signs, the patterns of activity, the coincidences—these are what make up the language of the spirit world that reaches out to connect with us. Sometimes we can piece these things together and develop an understanding about the spirit and why it's revealing itself to us. And other times, it's OK to never understand and to learn to surrender to the unknown and find peace in a parallel existence.

There are some general acceptances about why spirits haunt places. Maybe the spirit has unfinished business. Or perhaps a spirit wants to take care of a loved one or keep watch over a special place where he or she felt a sense of belonging. Maybe the spirit wants to deliver a message like "I'm OK, and you can move on," or "You're in danger." Some spirits may have died suddenly and don't realize they are dead. They may be trying to move to "the light" or cross over to the other side, but they're trapped. They need help. Sometimes spirits attach themselves to objects like jewelry, tools, books or a car. They travel with the object, even if it passed through a series of owners.

I believe that the spirit world is present in our midst. It's not up in the sky or out in the universe. Albert Einstein said that time is an illusion—that there is no such thing as time. We live a linear existence because our spirits are captive in an aging body. We notice the difference between yesterday, today and tomorrow because we know our days are limited and our bodies will eventually die.

But in the spirit world, there are no bodies so there is no time. The child spirit in the Atlantic Hotel in Berlin is living in the same moment that she lived in when she was bouncing her ball and riding her tricycle down the second-floor hallway. Dr. Purnell at the Atlantic Hotel in Ocean City is still inspecting the place, looking after guests, making sure everything is in order. He is still living in that moment when he was responsible. Time doesn't exist for Dr. Purnell or that little girl. They exist in a timeless realm where everything just "is."

So your mother who died twenty years ago isn't pining away for your father until he finally dies and goes to heaven to be with her. She is present now, as she was when she was alive and as she will be when they meet in the afterlife. She is in the moment. Everything is present at once. This understanding helps us reconcile how the ghosts of soldiers at Gettysburg seem to be forever walking that battlefield and how some spirits of hoteliers never stop serving customers or some merchant ghosts are never able to leave the store. They are all present in their own special moments, with their spirits living outside of time.

Everything is made up of energy—pulsating particles of moving energy—and this energy creates its own field. When people come together, their combined energy fields morph into a collective field that stands alone. This is why we tend to feel peaceful in a church, edgy in a courtroom and somber in a graveyard. Concentrated human emotion can shift or change the energy field in a place. When a loved one dies and a family is left in mourning, the energy field in the house changes. The sense of mourning and yearning for the lost loved one charges the energy field, and it is this field that keeps the spirit of the departed ever present in the house. It is the "spiritual electricity" that connects this world and the next.

Sudden death such as murder, suicide or accidental death burns a strong imprint on the energy field. Even greater shifts in energy occur when there is collective violence, like a battle or a natural disaster. Emotion changes the field. And it is this energy field that connects the two worlds. It becomes a portal that beings in both worlds can access. So a feisty spirit that doesn't want to be forgotten, a guardian spirit that still wants to protect a loved one, a bitter spirit that wants revenge or a troubled spirit that can't find peace in his eternal existence can access the energy field in a way that we in the mortal world can sense. And when we mortals have a special sense or advanced psychic ability, we can also access the field and experience the presence of the spirits.

Because Ocean City and Berlin were places of such high human emotion—the happy vacationer, the welcoming hotelier or innkeeper, the entertainers, the drummers, the wealthy elite, the humble farm hands and the children who grew up by the sea—the spiritual charge is quite potent, and the seaside ghosts have been present to many. Here are just a few stories of how the two worlds have mingled in these two special towns.

PART I
OCEAN CITY

Painted panel on Trimper's Menagerie Carousel.

THE ATLANTIC HOTEL

On July 4, 1875, the Atlantic Hotel opened in Ocean City. The idea of a grand hotel on the sandy shores of the barrier island east of Sinepuxent Bay was conceived by a group of Lower Eastern Shore businessmen who believed that by creating this seaside resort, they could not only grow their investment but also open a whole new revenue stream for the local economy rooted in tourism. They gathered investors, bought the land, laid out the town and named it Ocean City. Their vision was prophetic, as Ocean City certainly became a thriving tourist town. And their vision for a grand hotel in a seaside resort town paved the way for other visions and entrepreneurial dreams, and all of those dreams came together to shape a culture and a destination that attracts seven million visitors every year. These are visitors who expect to eat Thrasher's French fries and Dolle's candy, stroll the Boardwalk, ride Trimper's Menagerie Carousel and do all things fun that have become part of the Ocean City brand. The Atlantic Hotel marked the beginning of that dream. When it opened, it was the anchor—the axis on which the town would spin.

It was built in the Victorian style, four stories high with tall columns across the hotel's oceanfront façade. It could accommodate four hundred guests, and it stretched from Atlantic Avenue (the Boardwalk) to Baltimore Avenue—a full city block. This amazing structure was the only thing on the barrier island except for a few guest cottages and fishing camps. The rooms of the Atlantic Hotel were large and airy with excellent ventilation, according to a reporter from the *Salisbury Advertiser*. The hotel would meet

Postcard of the Atlantic Hotel, circa 1920.

all the visitors' needs and provide daily entertainment. There was a casino, a billiard room, a huge dining room and a dance hall with a first-class orchestra. Guests would have all three of their daily meals at the hotel, take in the seaside views and perhaps bathe in the ocean, stroll the Boardwalk or relax on the porches. This was at a time when cities were filthy with bulging populations and poor sanitation. Most people living on the west side of the Chesapeake Bay all the way to the Mississippi River would never see an ocean in their lifetimes. The Atlantic Ocean was something people only read about in books or heard about in stories. This new resort opened up opportunity for travel in a post–Civil War era when the American economy was being reshaped and people wanted to start feeling good again—to look to the future.

At first, people came by stagecoaches and ferries, but in 1878, the railroad was extended all the way to Sinepuxent Bay. Shortly after that, a bridge was built that allowed the train to stop near the front door of the Atlantic Hotel. Ocean City became a romantic, magical summertime destination that a family could reach in a half-day train ride.

Even with the railroad and the growing amenities around the Atlantic Hotel—such as smaller beach cottages, the Pier and Trimper's Amusements—the Atlantic Hotel had a hard time attracting customers and paying the bills. By 1913, the *Baltimore Sun* had printed an article that said the hotel was in such bad disrepair that it was set to be torn down. Instead of demolishing it, the owners sold it to the mayor of Ocean City and his partner. They promised to renovate it. By 1922, the nearly fifty-year-old dilapidated wooden structure had been purchased by one of the hotel's stockholders, a Dr. Charles W. Purnell. He devised a plan to bring the Atlantic Hotel back to its former glory.

Dr. Charles Washington Purnell (nicknamed "Wash") was the grandson of Isaac Coffin, the Worcester County farmer who erected the first rooming house for guests in Ocean City in 1869. Coffin's rooming house sat just a few blocks north of where the Atlantic Hotel was built, and after Isaac Coffin's death in 1892, his son Neil (Charles Purnell's uncle) continued to operate it under the name Ocean House. Neil Coffin produced the first set of picture postcards with views of Ocean City in 1904. So Charles Purnell came from a well-rooted family that was invested in the success of Ocean City as a tourist town.

Three years after Charles Purnell purchased and began renovations on the Atlantic Hotel, a devastating fire broke out in the electric plant just blocks away. It was such a cold December day that water was said to have frozen in the fire hoses. The fire consumed everything within three square blocks, including the Atlantic Hotel. Dr. Purnell had to begin again.

He directed construction of a new, bigger and better hotel immediately, and by the next summer, part of the hotel was open for receiving guests. Eventually, the Atlantic Hotel became an H-shaped structure with two wings and all the modern conveniences. According to the Purnell family, Dr. Purnell and his wife, Flossie, loved being hosts at the Atlantic Hotel. He spent most of the day in the lobby and prided himself on knowing every guest's name. He was gregarious and friendly and spent forty years running the hotel before his death in 1962.

Dr. Purnell's great-grandchildren run the Atlantic Hotel today, making them the fourth Purnell generation to be greeting guests. The hotel still has that family-run feel where the staff takes personal responsibility for making guests feel welcomed. Today, guests can lounge on the rooftop deck that overlooks the Atlantic Ocean, the beach and the Boardwalk, or they can walk directly out onto the famous Boardwalk from the wide hotel lobby. There's a heated pool, a large parking lot and an old elevator that still is in working order. Though the hotel retains its old-time character, every room has air-conditioning, a private bath and cable television.

If spirits come back to where they were most happy, then it makes sense that the Atlantic Hotel would house a few spirits—especially the

A view of the Atlantic Hotel in Ocean City today.

ghost of Dr. Purnell. According to the staff at the Atlantic Hotel, he was a tall, thin man with a long face and thinning hair. He was bald on top, and he wore round spectacles. He always wore a jacket and tie. And this description fits what staff and guests have said they've seen over the years—in a man who appears in mirrors, vanishes in hallways, stands in corners and is seen looking out windows. Why is that strange? Because one common feature in all the apparitions of this man is that he vanishes before their eyes. He looks real and seems real, but then he walks through a door or wall or just dissolves.

The lobby of the Atlantic Hotel is beautiful, decorated with bright fabrics, comfortable sofas and chairs and upper-class accents. At the end of the lobby, on the wall bordering the Boardwalk, is a seven-foot-tall mirror framed in dark wood. On either side of it are two upholstered chairs. According to hotel staff, this mirror was original to the first Atlantic Hotel, as is the wood table by the door that exits onto the Boardwalk. Occasionally, people see a shadow in this mirror when they are walking toward it. Sometimes it's small, like a child. Sometimes the shadow takes on the features of Dr. Purnell. And sometimes it's not a shadow at all but a full-blown apparition of a little child or of a man with a long face, a balding head and round spectacles.

The double doors that once led into the grand dining hall are opposite the mirror. Since the dining room is no longer in use, the area is now used for storage and is accessible only to hotel staff. Several staff members are keenly aware that they are most likely to see an apparition in that mirror when they are coming through those doors. Some suspect the doors are some kind of portal. One staff member who works nights says she knocks on the door before she goes through it just to let the spirits know she's there, and she never looks into the mirror. Others report that they'll see their own reflections along with a shadow figure behind them. One staff member described it to me this way: "Sometimes you see a shadow in the reflection, just like a shadow on the wall, but when you turn around to see who the shadow belongs to, there's no one there."

A staff person who works security shared how he would see Dr. Purnell from time to time. He'd see him every once in awhile near the exit to an upper-floor balcony that closed at midnight. A man who works security would see a guy walking down the hallway after midnight, moving toward

The mirror in the lobby of the Atlantic Hotel. This piece was rescued from the first Atlantic Hotel, which burned down in 1925.

the balcony door. He'd call out to the guy, saying the balcony was closed, and the man would turn the corner and disappear. Just enough time would go by for the security man to forget about it when it would happen again. He believes the man who vanishes is Dr. Purnell. A dormered window was positioned where that balcony stands today. Dr. Purnell loved to look out that window.

The same security guy also remarked about how calls from guest rooms would come in to the front desk, and when the clerk answered, there would be no one on the other end of the phone line. The clerk would call the room back, and there would still be no answer. Then the clerk would check who was in the room, and there would be no one registered. The staff began noticing that when this happened, it seemed to be a warning that something in or around the room was malfunctioning—a water backup, a broken air conditioner, an electrical problem. It didn't happen often, but it was strangely coincidental that when they'd get a phantom call from one of these vacant rooms, the room would soon turn up with a problem that needed attention.

An electrician who works in the hotel said he's seen Dr. Purnell on the stairway leading from the front desk to the second floor. He said the stairway was always an active site for spirits when he worked in the hotel in the off-season, when everything was closed up for the winter and he was the only one in the building. He described seeing not only Dr. Purnell on the stairway but also an African American man dressed like an entertainer in old-time clothing wearing a zoot suit with high-waisted pants and a long jacket.

A few years back, a man descended that same staircase and told the desk clerk he had to check out right away. He seemed agitated and gave the clerk his key. The clerk noticed that he had a very old key—the kind with the room number printed on it. The hotel didn't use this style key anymore. He said he had booked for the entire week but he had to leave right away. As the clerk started to pull up his information on the computer, he walked out the front door and into the parking lot. The clerk saw that the room was booked for the week. She instructed housekeeping staff to go and clean the room. Housekeeping came back and explained that an entire family was in the room, and all of their stuff was still there. The man who had turned in the key was never booked in that room. How did he get the key? This became quite a mystery, and the hotel staff tried to figure out where this man came from and what room he was in. They interviewed the family who was in the room that he "checked out of," and they had no idea who this phantom guest was. They'd had no visitors, and there was no one in the room except

The stairway at the Atlantic Hotel where spirits are often seen.

those who had originally checked in. No guest or staff member had noticed this man or seen him in the hotel at all except the clerk who received his key at the desk.

Because of the mysterious nature of the incident, especially because the phantom guest had a working (though old) key in his possession, the hotel staff notified the police. When the clerk gave her description of the man to the police, she realized that the man had no identifying marks—nothing that distinguished him from most young men. She described him as a white male, average height, with dark brown hair and blue eyes, wearing blue jeans, a white shirt and white athletic shoes. He had no belt, no watch, no tattoos, no mustache, no facial hair, no glasses, no hat or ball cap and nothing that would set him apart. The same clerk shared how a few weeks later she was on the phone with her sister who had just had a terrible nightmare. Her sister explained that she dreamed that she got out of bed and walked past the mirror in her bedroom, but when she looked in the mirror, it wasn't her own reflection looking back. It was the reflection of a young man. It startled her and left her with an uneasy feeling. The clerk asked her sister what the man looked like, and her sister offered almost the same description that the clerk had given the police a few weeks before: he was a white male with blue eyes and dark hair wearing a white shirt and jeans but no other identifying marks.

The police never located the guy, and no one at the hotel ever saw him again. No one could offer any explanation about where the key came from.

The same electrician who saw Dr. Purnell on the stairway said he had other mysterious experiences in the hotel during the winter when he was the only one in the building. He explained that during the winter the doors to guest rooms are left open. As he walked down the halls, he'd occasionally see someone in a room out of the corner of his eye. But when he'd look directly at the image, it would vanish. There were days when he'd walk down a hallway and catch multiple glimpses of guests in rooms in his peripheral vision. He learned to ignore it, as he learned to ignore the one rocking chair on the second-floor deck that didn't rock. While all the other rockers were swaying in the wind, one lone rocker on the end would be still. The electrician also noticed cold spots in parts of the hotel, particularly on the main stairway, and one day when he was working on the elevator, he noticed shoe prints on the top of the elevator. He couldn't begin to explain how someone could access the open shaft and then put their feet on the top of the car.

When doing wiring in the attic, the electrician explained, he accessed the attic through a door in the ceiling. He'd stand on a chair and then lift himself through. One day, he was working in the attic and needed a tool from his truck. He descended through the ceiling door to the chair and then to the floor, and then he retrieved his tool. He was the only person in the building that day. Or so he thought. When he returned to the attic, he saw that his chair had been moved. It was relocated to a place up against the wall instead of being in the middle of the hall where he left it. He assumed it was just the spirit of Dr. Purnell watching out for things.

Paranormal experts say that spirits suck energy out of the environment in order to manifest themselves in the living world. The orb is the beginning. Drawing more energy from the environment, a spirit can manifest itself as a shadow or milky-white mist, and with even more energy—the most energy—a spirit can present itself as a full-blown apparition. This explains why batteries are drained and electric lights and appliances malfunction when spirits are present. They are drawing energy out of the environment. The electrician and a few of his helpers brought cameras to work one day. They began shooting pictures near where they were working. It was the off-season, and the hotel was empty. They were amazed at the number of pictures they took that had orbs, strange lights, misty white spots and shadows.

It seems that the spirits of the Atlantic Hotel present themselves mostly to the staff and those doing contract work. But there are a few guests who have reported some interesting occurrences. A female guest who was staying with her husband in a double room with two beds told the hotel staff that while she was asleep, she was awakened by something tickling her feet. She assumed it was her husband, but she glanced over to the next bed and saw that he was in it sound asleep. Another guest reported that she woke up and saw a little girl standing next to a man dressed in uniform—like the uniform of a sailor. She said they were as clear to her as any human being would be. At first she thought the two must have stumbled into the wrong room, but then she noticed that they were wearing old-time clothes. She turned to her sleeping husband to wake him up, and when she looked back to the corner where they were standing, they were gone.

All of the spirits of the Atlantic Hotel are happy. Nothing scary or awful has ever been reported. The staff and contract workers who have experienced these unexplained events believe that the spirits are there because they were happy there, and spirits and humans alike are all part of the Atlantic Hotel family. The good times of past and present mingle to create the warm welcome that greets every guest at the Atlantic Hotel. Those spirits are coming back to a place of memory—a place where they recall the happiest times of their lives. Most believe Dr. Purnell is present because he's still taking care of things, still seeing that his guests are comfortable and enjoying themselves. The fact that his family is still at the helm and running his beloved hotel keeps him close both in their memories and in the spirit world. That connection and the act of being fondly remembered keep him present.

So if you're ever at the Atlantic Hotel in Ocean City, why not wander into the lobby and take in the atmosphere. Become a part of the mystique—the environment of two worlds lovingly knitted together.

THE OCEAN CITY
LIFE-SAVING STATION MUSEUM

Between 1847 and 1878, the U.S. Congress established and funded the U.S. Life-Saving Service (LSS) to render assistance from the shore to the victims of shipwrecks. Life-saving stations were established up and down the East Coast. Ocean City still has a restored life-saving station that was built in 1891, and it serves as a museum and repository for artifacts and manuscripts that tell Ocean City's history. It is located at the end of the Boardwalk at the Inlet, and it houses over ten thousand artifacts, six thousand photographs and three thousand postcards.

A life-saving station would have employed a keeper and six surfmen. By day, they would scan the horizon for distressed ships from the tower, and by night, the surfmen would take turns patrolling the beach either on foot or on horseback. There was a life-saving station about every ten miles along the Delmarva coastline, and the efforts of all of these stations together provided a complete surveillance of the shoreline.

At the station house, there were sleeping quarters on the second floor and a watchtower above that. When the surfmen spotted a ship in distress, they broke into action. There were several modes of rescue—all were dangerous. One method of rescue was to row out to the ship in a long, open boat known as a surfboat. Several men could fit in it, and they could pull a few more on board. They would have to wheel the boat down onto the beach, work at getting it launched and then push it out to sea through the crashing waves. In bad weather (common during shipwrecks), this could be particularly difficult, and the danger of capsizing and drowning grew as they moved

An Ocean City Life-Saving Station Museum postcard view.

farther out to sea. Another means of rescue was to use a cannon to shoot a rope out to the wrecked ship with an apparatus called a Breeches Buoy tied to the end of the rope. It looked like a round life preserver ring with short pants (breeches) sewn into the ring. A person aboard the shipwreck could put his legs through the breeches and securely float as if standing up in the water. Those who were stranded would grab the rope and pull it toward themselves until they could retrieve the Breeches Buoy. Then, one at a time, they would climb into it and be reeled into the shore by the surfmen. A third process was the Life-Car, a capsule-shaped metal container that could hold two to three people lying down. This was used for shipwrecks that were only a few hundred yards out to sea. It employed the same concept as the Breeches Buoy, but three people would lie down in the metal capsule, close the hatch and then be pulled through the crashing sea by surfmen on shore.

The Ocean City Life-Saving Station Museum's website has a collection of true shipwreck stories describing in detail how the surfmen came to the rescue of stranded mariners and the challenges they faced. The museum also has actual life-saving equipment, including the surfboat, the Breeches Buoy and the Life-Car.

Formerly, the life-saving station building was up the beach at Caroline Street. Eventually, the U.S. Coast Guard took over the life-saving efforts and occupied the building until 1964, when it built a more modern structure near the Inlet. The building, which was owned by the town, fell into disrepair and was used on and off for various departments until the town decided to demolish it in 1977. A group of citizens who wanted to preserve the building and its history intervened and protested the demolition. The Ocean City Museum Society was formed, and it partnered with the town to move the building to its present location and raise funds to restore it so that it could be used as a museum. The station house was dedicated officially as a museum on Christmas Day 1978.

Today, the museum not only has one of the finest collections of life-saving equipment in the United States, but it also has artifacts that chronicle Ocean City's history, an aquarium, a collection of sands from around the world and the original logbook written by the station house keeper with the first entry on December 26, 1878.

There are displays on the history of the Boardwalk that include the old rolling wicker chairs, kewpie dolls and a seat from the Boardwalk's original Ferris wheel.

One of the artifacts on display from the Boardwalk is "Laughing Sal." This is an oversized mannequin-like rag doll that once stood upright in a wire cage at the entrance of Jester's Funhouse on Worcester Street at the Boardwalk. Sal had a huge papier-mâché face that resembled a clown's with painted-on arched eyebrows; puffy, rouge-colored cheeks; and a bright-red open mouth exposing an eerie smile with one front tooth missing. She wore a

Laughing Sal, a life-size doll that laughs, is now housed at the Life-Saving Station Museum.

wig and hat and a print dress with a jacket and had a large pocketbook slung over her shoulder. Her black Mary Jane shoes were painted on because her feet were too large to accommodate real shoes.

And if Sal wasn't spooky enough just to look at, she also moved and laughed. The Jesters, who were the owners of the arcade, would operate electronic controls behind a concession stand that made Laughing Sal move and laugh. At just the right time, they'd pull the right levers that would make Laughing Sal shake her head and wave her arms and then let out a cackling laugh that was projected through a loudspeaker. Author John Barth mentions her in his short story "Lost in the Funhouse" but refers to her as "Fat May":

> *Larger than life, Fat May mechanically shook, rocked on her heels, slapped her thighs while recorded laughter—uproarious, female—came amplified from a hidden loudspeaker. It chuckled, wheezed, wept; tried in vain to catch its breath; tittered, groaned, exploded raucous and anew.*

People say that you couldn't help laughing when you heard Laughing Sal let out that crazy laugh. But to some, the sound was eerie. It was startling—and that was the point. People on the Boardwalk who heard the laugh would come to see what it was and hopefully enter the arcade and spend some money. Laughing Sal was a sort of possessed, animatronic rag doll in a cage that laughed like a cackling witch in order to attract attention. Many people in their sixties who visited Ocean City as children remember seeing Laughing Sal. She was certainly the most memorable part of the funhouse.

After the Jesters sold their funhouse, Laughing Sal was stored in a building behind their property. Vandals broke in and damaged Laughing Sal—ripping the dress, stealing a hand and mashing the face. It was a great loss. Later, Mrs. Jester gave what remained of Laughing Sal to the Ocean City Life-Saving Station Museum, and it lovingly restored this Boardwalk icon.

Today, Laughing Sal resides behind glass on the second floor of the museum. She has new hair, hat and dress, and her face has been repaired. She doesn't move anymore, but she does laugh—that same old cackling laugh. Now there's a button on the front of the glass that museum visitors can press, and it will call forth that crazy laugh that comes in two sweeps. It is very loud and echoes throughout the building.

But this Laughing Sal has a mind of her own. The museum staff will all admit that sometimes she laughs all by herself when no one is pressing the button. Often times, no one is even present on the second floor. One staff member explained that Laughing Sal seems to laugh on her own during creepy weather, like when there's a storm or when the wind is whistling past the museum or the rain is battering the walls and windows. Laughing Sal either really hates or really loves bad weather because it tends to bring the laugh even though no one is at the controls.

A museum guest said that when she pressed the button, nothing happened—no laugh. She pressed it again, and there was still no laugh. Then she gave up. She spent about twenty minutes looking at all of the second-floor displays and then proceeded down the stairs. When she was halfway down the staircase, old Laughing Sal started. She let out that big cackling laugh. The guest stopped and listened, waiting until Sal finished. The she proceeded down the stairs thinking she'd tell the museum staff what happened. The guest reached the first floor and turned to go back into the gift shop; as soon as she was about to tell the shop clerk what happened, Laughing Sal started to laugh again. The shop clerk admitted there were no other guests or staff in the building.

There are some who believe that spirits can attach themselves to things—sentimental items, tools, books, art, photographs or a favorite toy. Wherever the item goes, the spirit follows. This is why many museums and antique stores often have that haunted feel. Who knows why Laughing Sal laughs at will. One could explain it as an electrical short or not. Sensitive people—people who can feel spirits about them—will say Laughing Sal has a spirit attached to her. And that spirit makes her laugh.

Spiritually sensitive people—psychics and mediums—have come into the museum and told staff there that they have felt cold spots in the museum, particularly in the boat room. Others have said they sense the spirit of a child in the building. Several occurrences in the museum suggest that they might be correct. Miss Betty, a longtime staff member at the museum who is now retired, recalled a few experiences she had during her years working there. She said that sometimes people would say they felt like a child was following them, walking behind them, but when they turned to look at the child, no one was there.

Once, the stairs to the watchtower were being painted, and museum staff had to stay off them for a few days until the paint dried. The museum keeps supplies up in the tower, and a staff member went up to retrieve some just a few days after the stairs had been painted. That staff person noticed the imprint of a little shoe on the top step. It wasn't there before the stairs were painted, and there weren't two shoes—just one. There was no blemish in the paint on the steps where the small shoe would have picked up the paint needed to make the imprint. The people who worked in the museum at the time saw the footprint and were perplexed. No one had an explanation.

Miss Betty recalled that one day, she and another staff person, Richard, were about to close the museum. Richard had locked all the doors to the museum except the front door, and the two of them sat in the gift shop area near the front door waiting until it was time to close and go home. A little boy came bolting through the front door and ran past them. Miss Betty described him as the most beautiful child she had ever seen. He was about five years old with blond hair, blue eyes and a green shirt. Richard and Miss Betty were expecting his parents to walk in after him, but no one came in. So Richard decided to go find the child, ask him where his parents were and place him safely in his parents' care before they closed.

Richard couldn't find the boy anywhere. He knew the child couldn't have gotten out any of the other doors because he'd locked them. The only way out was the way in, and the child would have had to pass Betty in order to get out. Miss Betty remained in the gift shop while Richard searched. He looked in every room—in the closets, in the tower. He even looked inside the big surfboat and Life-Car to see if the child had crawled into one of them. The little boy had vanished. And after searching every square foot of the museum with no trace of the boy, Richard and Betty went home.

Richard also recalled being on the second floor and hearing someone call his name—"Richard! Richard!"—from the bottom of the steps. He went to the steps and replied, "Yes?" but there was no one there. Richard asked Sonja, who was working in the gift shop, if she heard someone calling him. She heard it, too, but didn't see anyone come in or leave the museum and didn't recognize the voice.

One other strange occurrence involved the Life-Car mentioned previously. The distressed would climb inside the Life-Car, lie down and then close the hatch behind them. The surfmen on the shore would pull the Life-Car through the crashing waves, bringing the car's occupants to safety. A Life-Car that was used in local shipwreck rescues is on display in the museum's boat room. One day, a young man came into the museum and explained to Miss Betty that he was a contractor and would be traveling soon to Kuwait. He asked Miss Betty if she would like him to bring back some sand from Kuwait to go in their "Sands from Around the World" exhibit. She replied that they would appreciate that and would welcome the sand to put in their display. When the man returned with the sand, he asked if it would be OK if he brought his mother in to see the sand and the rest of the museum, and Miss Betty said that his mother was very welcome to come in.

The Life-Car was used for rescuing up to three people at a time from a distressed ship.

He returned with his mother, and the two began a leisurely walk through the museum's exhibits. But they left in a hurry, and Miss Betty didn't get a chance to say goodbye to them. But the young man came back a few months later and told Miss Betty what had happened. He said that his mother felt a rush of cold air when she entered the boat room—so cold that it felt like a freezer door had been opened. She was reading the signage about the Life-Car, and when she finished, she went over to look inside the car. When she looked inside, she saw a drowned sailor lying on the bottom of the car. He was gray—and dead. He was wearing a black slicker and a hat, and his hair was all mashed to his face. The slicker and hair were covered with seawater; in fact, she said that she could smell the seawater and hear the water droplets dripping from the top of the Life-Car. It all happened in seconds, but the vision was so vivid—taking in her senses of sight, sound and smell. She let out an audible gasp and felt faint. Her son rushed over to her and asked her what was wrong. She asked him to take her outside, which he quickly did. She was almost freezing when she hit the warm air on the Boardwalk, and she told her son what she saw. The young man explained all this to Miss Betty and said his mother would surely never be back.

Why would a child, a sailor or others haunt a place like the Ocean City Life-Saving Station Museum? It's a place associated with life and death. The equipment, the building itself, the watchtower—all of these things were created for responding to life-threatening emergencies. No doubt, people came close to losing their lives in that Life-Car, and perhaps some were dead when it was reeled in after certain rescues. Perhaps a child lost his life in a rescue.

Or spirits might be attached to the many artifacts housed in the museum. Perhaps a child or children were happiest when they were listening to Laughing Sal cackle or when they were riding on the Ferris wheel. Perhaps a favorite toy was one of the kewpie dolls that are on display. Spirits can attach themselves to things or return to places where they were happy, and sometimes a spirit is trapped when the body dies quickly, as in an accident like a drowning. All of these are possible reasons why the Ocean City Life-Saving Station Museum remains one of the most pleasantly haunted places in Ocean City.

TRIMPER'S MENAGERIE CAROUSEL

In 1890, Daniel Trimper, a German immigrant, and his wife, Margaret, the daughter of German immigrants, sold their popular Baltimore bar known as the Silver Dollar and moved to Ocean City to operate an amusement park they had purchased. The park had two hotels on it and was located between South Division and South First Streets. The Trimpers renovated the property and rebuilt one of the hotels to look like Windsor Castle. Later, they added a movie theater and indoor rides. Now, the complex has only the Inlet Lodge as a hotel, but the property has expanded to include outdoor rides, arcades, concessions and stores. And the Trimper name is famous in Ocean City. Daniel Trimper ran the operation for forty years until his death in 1929. He and Margaret had ten children, seven of whom reached adulthood. Their descendants—now in the fifth generation—continue to operate Trimper Rides and Amusements, which is now a multimillion-dollar corporation. They also continue to offer leadership and service in the Ocean City community.

One of the most memorable Trimpers was Granville, who took over management of the company in 1980. Referred to as a "jolly old man" by his grandson Chris, Granville was not only loved by his family but also had a high profile in the community, serving for eighteen years on the Ocean City Council, including a term as president. In the year 2000, the Ocean City Chamber of Commerce elected him Citizen of the Year. He was a character that embodied the Trimper spirit.

A 1920s woodcarving of a fairy that tops an old ticket booth in the Trimper's Carousel Building.

Staff members who operate the outdoor rides at Trimper's tell about strange events that have happened in the Trimper's Lodge basement. It seems that the lodge had a casino on the bottom level, and it was a hot spot in town. Trimper's staff says that there are rooms now where the casino was, and every once in a while, they'll catch a glimpse of someone who looks like Granville. And on that bottom floor, broken things have a way of fixing themselves. A guest might call about a television that doesn't work, or a leak in the bathroom or a problem with the phone, but when a technician arrives to fix the problem, everything suddenly works fine. Two staff members casually commented, "It's just old Granville fixing things before we get there." Some of the Trimper's staff members feel the strong presence of Granville throughout the establishment, but especially in the lodge. It is a benevolent presence.

The Trimper's Menagerie Carousel "Forever Joanne" horse was named in memory of Joanne Trimper.

Probably the most famous ride at Trimper's is the menagerie carousel that has forty-eight hand-carved animals, three chariots and a rocking chair. Daniel Trimper purchased it from the Herschell-Spellman Company, located in New York, and it was put in place in 1912 and has stood on that same spot ever since—even when the Atlantic Ocean waters eclipsed the horses' knees during large storms. It is the oldest continually operating carousel in America. Every animal is unique, carved by German master carvers, and each is a separate, beautiful, priceless work of art. Besides the variety of horses, there is a mule, a giraffe, a lion, a tiger, a sea monster, a zebra, a ram, a rooster, a stork, a chicken, a pig, an ostrich, a frog, a cat, a dog, a deer and a camel, making it a menagerie of carousel animals. Trimper's keeps a mechanic and restoration artist on staff just to maintain the antique rides that are housed in the carousel building.

The carousel has two levels and brightly painted panels on the center column and ceilings. There was a time when all of it was painted green. In the 1970s, the Trimpers invested in a major restoration of the carousel. It was then that a Ukrainian brother-and-sister team—the restoration artists—discovered all of the artwork under that green paint. They took on the tedious task of removing each layer of paint until they revealed the original artist renderings of young horse riders reaching for the brass ring and women in beach clothing of the early twentieth century.

The word "carousel" is linked to the Italian word *carosello*, which means "little war." Carosello was actually a war game played in the twelfth century. The purpose was to improve the skills of potential soldiers in horse riding. Men would ride bareback on horses and toss scented balls that had been dunked in perfume to one another. The goal was to catch the ball. Riders who missed were doused with perfume when the ball hit the ground and broke on impact beneath them. Later, the same game was adopted by the French and expanded to include spearing a ring that was hung from a post or a tree—the origin of the phrase "grab the brass ring." The French created a practice machine that placed fake horses on a rotating platform that was turned by men or horses. This practice machine became popular with children and women and eventually morphed into the carousel.

The Italian carosello game where losers are doused in perfume has an interesting connection to a current Trimper carousel ghost story.

A woman who has worked at Trimper's for over thirty years shared an experience about the Trimper carousel having a funny smell. The mechanic who worked on the antique rides came to her about seven years ago and said there was a strange smell around the carousel. He wondered if they had changed any of the chemicals they were using. The woman checked all the past invoices and noted that there were no new products or chemicals being used for the carousel. About seven months later, when the carousel house was closed for the season and only a skeleton staff was present in the Trimper complex, the antique ride artist approached this same woman, saying she smelled something strange around the carousel. This piqued the woman's interest because the carousel building was closed. There wasn't a possibility that a smell was wafting in from other business out on the Boardwalk. The woman approached the carousel herself and couldn't smell a thing. She dismissed the thought.

About three weeks later, Trimper's was still closed for the off-season, and the woman was walking by the carousel when she smelled something different. No one was around. The smell was familiar, but she couldn't identify it. Shortly after, she was with her granddaughter testing perfumes at the Boscov's perfume counter, and all of a sudden, she smelled that scent again—the same one she'd smelled near the carousel. She looked at the bottom of the perfume bottle. It said, "Cristal." She remembered that name. It was the name of the perfume that Joanne Trimper wore.

Joanne Morgan was born in Sharptown, Maryland, a town on the Nanticoke River in Wicomico County. The volunteer fire department in Sharptown has operated a carnival there since 1926. The carnival intended to lease a ride from Trimper's, so Granville Trimper hauled the ride to Sharptown. It was during that trip that he met Joanne Morgan. They fell in love and were married. Joanne and Granville made their life in Ocean City, and she worked alongside him at Trimper's until she died at the young age of sixty-two. Granville took his beloved wife back to Sharptown to be buried, and when he died seventeen years later, he was buried next to her.

Joanne loved the carousel, and according to the Trimper family, her favorite horse was the white horse with deep red roses decked with a turquoise sash. It sits on the outside ring and is a stunning work of art. Joanne would occasionally ride the carousel and talked about it often, encouraging guests not to miss taking a ride on it. And when she died, the Trimper family named her favorite horse "Forever Joanne" in her memory. Granville also had the Trimper carousel etched onto her grave memorial with her horse front and center.

As the author of this book and the teller of many ghost stories, I seldom have a personal experience at one of the sites, but the Trimper carousel was different. I took my twin eight-year-old granddaughters, Grace and Mia, with me to Ocean City when I was researching this book. They had heard the story of Joanne Trimper and the carousel. I had some interviews to do near the Inlet, and they wanted to ride the rides at Trimper's. So we got in line—a line that stretched right out in front of the carousel. Mia was distracted, but Grace and I were watching the carousel go around while we stood in line. I was thinking about Joanne Trimper and how easy it would be to love this carousel. I didn't know it, but Gracie was thinking about the story as well. All of a sudden, we smelled it. It was brief but strong—a flower-like scent that floated right past us. Just as I was trying to tell myself it had to be some woman standing near me (there were no women standing near me), Grace hollered out, "I smell it! I smell it! Joanne! I smell her perfume." I smiled, and Mia tried desperately to smell something, but she couldn't.

Later, I convinced myself that what we smelled at the carousel had to be someone nearby and not some phantom spirit. The next year, my daughter and I took my grandson to Trimper's and put him on the carousel. As I was watching him go around, I was remembering his mother being on that same carousel and having a little moment of nostalgia. The carousel does that to

The graves of Granville and Joanne Trimper in Sharptown, Maryland.

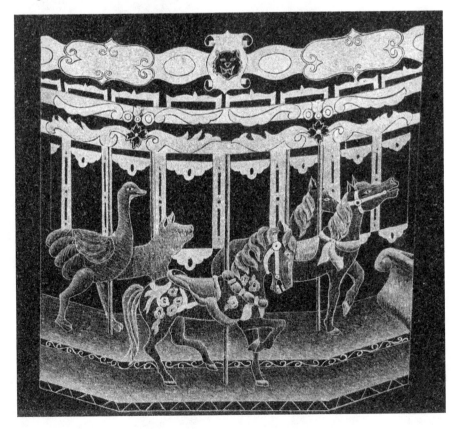

A close-up of the carousel engraved on the Trimper marker.

you. There's a magical quality to it. The colors, the animals, the children, the music, the painted panels—all of it creates this magic that wraps itself around you. No wonder Joanne Trimper loved this thing, and no wonder she might want to return here. I closed my eyes and tried to sense her presence and maybe catch a whiff of that perfume.

I couldn't. Nothing came to me. But then I said out loud, "C'mon, Joanne," and it came. That same scent floated right past me. I'm a believer now, and I'll never walk past the Trimper Rides and not think of her and that beautiful carousel.

THE HENRY HOTEL

Before the United States Congress passed the Civil Rights Act in 1964, African Americans were not permitted to stay in the same hotels as Caucasians, or use the same public bathrooms or eat in the same restaurants. In Ocean City, African Americans were also excluded from the Boardwalk and the ocean beaches. There was a designated beach on Sinepuxent Bay for "colored" people during the "Colored Excursion Days" when, after the summer season was concluded, blacks were invited into town to vacation. But the whites-only designations still applied in the hotels and restaurants—the ones that were still open.

The African American population was important to Ocean City, however, because they were a large part of the workforce. Many would come to town for the summer and work in the hotels and restaurants, but they would have to find lodging at "colored" establishments. The same applied to black entertainers. Louis Armstrong and Duke Ellington played at dance halls, ballrooms and some of the large hotels throughout the summer, but they would not be allowed to stay in those hotels overnight.

Colored hotels and rooming houses existed all over Ocean City, primarily to house the African American workforce. Only one of those hotels still stands: the Henry Hotel, a three-story, twenty-room hotel built in 1895 by Caucasian investors in order to support the need for housing black seasonal workers. It stayed in operation until 2003. The hotel is still maintained and owned by the Bonner family, though it is not open to guests.

Henry's Colored Hotel, built to accommodate African American guests during the times of segregation.

In 1926, an African American mail carrier named Charles T. Henry and his wife, Louisa, bought the hotel and renamed it Henry's Colored Hotel. The Henrys engaged the black community and offered a spirit of entertainment to their guests rather than mere beds for the night. They added a restaurant and a laundry and eventually put in a nightclub across the street that had gambling and entertainment. The nightclub was called the Grand Terrace and catered to both black and white guests. Over the years, the Henrys welcomed many black entertainers as guests, including Cab Calloway, Duke Ellington, Louis Armstrong, Willie Harmon, Count Basie and a very young James Brown.

The entire hotel is about the size of most single-family homes found in upscale suburban neighborhoods. The Henry has been out of commission since its most recent owner, Pearl Bonner, died in 2003. Ms. Bonner purchased the hotel in 1964. She was a single African American woman from Baltimore who was raising three daughters at the time. For forty summers, she ran the hotel with the help of her daughters, who in the early years were also working in town to earn money to put toward their college educations. Pearl ran the hotel as a rooming house for African American men who worked in Ocean City. She also built a loose-knit community around the hotel and its patrons.

The Edward H. Nabb Research Center at Salisbury University houses a Folklore Collection that includes transcribed oral commentary given to university students in the 1970s. There are thousands of pages of commentary in the collection, including stories of ghosts and hauntings. There is one piece of commentary about the Henry Hotel. It is short—fewer than 150 words—given by a male African American informant in 1973. He was sixty-one years old at the time. He lived in Berlin but worked year-round in Ocean City as a maintenance man. He said in his commentary that he had to walk past the Henry Hotel in the evenings when he'd catch his ride home.

The informant said that in the summertime, he had no issues with walking past the hotel. But when winter set in, the town was closed up and had only a few people on the streets. The Inlet area was like a ghost town, and walking the streets at night down there was a lonely ordeal. He said when he walked past the Henry Hotel, he would hear what sounded like faint music and laughing coming from inside. He could see that the hotel was empty, closed for the winter. There were no lights on or visual signs of any occupants. But there was music playing, and it seemed to be coming from there. He walked up closer to the building trying hard to hear where it was coming from, but the closer he got to the building, the more faint and distorted the music became. When he stepped on the grass in front of the house, the music stopped. But it started again as he walked away from the hotel. This happened several times—always with the same result. It bothered the man so much that he changed his walking route. He said, "That place has something going on in it that's not…not right."

I interviewed a West Ocean City resident who said that he once worked as a contractor for the Henry Hotel in the off-season. He was doing some inside repair work. He said, "It was a strange place. Like it was empty but not empty." He was hesitant to elaborate but said he couldn't leave fast enough.

Today, the Henry Hotel is well maintained. Though it is a modest building, its trim is painted and it has fresh screen on the wraparound porch and a white picket fence enclosing the front yard. The Lower Eastern Shore Heritage Council has designated the hotel an African American Heritage site, and the Bonner family wants to keep the hotel and perhaps reopen it as a venue that will memorialize their mother and contributions of African Americans in Ocean City.

I walked out to the Henry Hotel to take photographs one day, and a man sitting at the adjacent bus stop asked me what I was doing. We began a conversation, and he told me about an experience he had at the Henry Hotel. He said he worked in the off-season at the Inlet. For one job, he'd have to walk right past the Henry Hotel. He knew it was vacant, but one night, he saw someone on the screened porch looking at him. He said it was very late—and weird to see someone there. When he looked closer, he saw he was mistaken. No one was there. But it happened another time, and that time he was sure he saw someone or something on the porch over on the side facing the bus station. But when he took a closer look, there was nothing there. He said he always felt like someone was watching him from the porch.

A few days later, I came across an article online about the Henry Hotel. My friend Chris Guy, a reporter at the *Baltimore Sun*, wrote "Summers Apart," dated May 4, 2007. In the article, he traced the history of the Henry Hotel and included personal commentary taken from his interviews with Pearl Bonner's daughters.

A line from the article read:

> *Pearl Bonner was a resolute innkeeper, accepting only male borders and insisting they return for the night by 2:00 am. Often, her daughters say, she would wait up and see that they did.*

As a note of interest, next door to the Henry Hotel is a blue house. This was one of the old fishing camps that accommodated fishermen who came to Ocean City for fishing excursions. Their stay would include lodging and meals. It is also the house that was used on the set of the Columbia Pictures movie *Violets Are Blue*, starring Sissy Spacek and Kevin Kline, filmed in 1986.

TARRY-A-WHILE GUEST HOUSE

B uilt around 1895, the Tarry-A-While was a three-story guest house with thirteen rooms that could accommodate twenty-five guests. Thomas and Sallie Cropper, who both came from northern Worcester County farming families, owned the property and operated it as a guest house until their deaths. The family continued the operation for over one hundred years. Originally, the Tarry-A-While was located on Dorchester between the Boardwalk and Baltimore Avenue. In 2004, it was in a state of disrepair and slated to be demolished. The Town of Ocean City moved it one block west to the corner of Dorchester Street and Philadelphia Avenue, and with the assistance of the Ocean City Development Corporation, which is now housed in the Tarry-A-While, it obtained grants to restore the structure to its former solid condition. Today, the restored Tarry-A-While is one of the best existing examples of the early Ocean City guest houses.

Thomas and Sallie Cropper had seven children and raised them all at Tarry-A-While. The family occupied the rooms on the first floor and rented all of the rooms on the upper floors. If it was an especially busy summer season, the family might all move into one room—putting cots in the living room, laundry room and porches for themselves—and rent out the first-floor bedrooms to guests.

Tarry-A-While was the first guest house in Ocean City to advertise "Running Water in Every Room," which actually meant there was a sink in every room. Guests still had to share one bathroom, but the sinks were a nice touch. In his article "The Tarry-A-While Guest House," Arthur T. Davis,

Tarry-A-While Guest House was the first in Ocean City to advertise running water in every room. *Image courtesy of the Maryland Historical Trust.*

who grew up in Tarry-A-While, states, "There was only one bathroom to go around. For ventilation there was a small window above each door. The guests were given a key to their rooms, but each one was a skeleton key that would open every door in the house. I don't remember any complaints." Arthur Davis was the son of Violet Cropper, who was the daughter of Thomas and Sallie. His article appears on the Ocean City Life-Saving Station Museum's website, in its Memories of Life on a Sandbar collection.

There is one account of Tarry-A-While being haunted in the Folklore Collection at the Edward H. Nabb Research Center. The informant stated that her family stayed at Tarry-A-While every summer that she could remember. They looked forward to it and would never consider staying anywhere else. But she recalled two things. When the nights were particularly hot, guests would go onto the porches and rock in the rocking chairs. Occasionally, there would be a rocker or two that weren't being used, and they'd notice that one empty rocker would rock by itself. There could be several chairs on the porch that were vacant, but one would always rock on its own. They called it the ghost of Tarry-A-While. The other thing she noted was that there was often the smell of cigarette smoke on the first floor, and the management would remind everyone that smoking was to be done outside only. She never thought much about it, but she remembered her parents, who were nonsmokers, commenting about how the management couldn't figure out who was smoking and how there were no traces left behind like cigarette butts or ashes on the floor.

I mentioned this folklore commentary to my sister, who also stayed at Tarry-A-While every year. She had never heard about the cigarette smoke, but she confirmed the rocker story. She said sometimes several rockers would be going by themselves, even when the night was so still there wasn't a hint of a breeze in the air.

The third memory from Tarry-A-While came from a woman who grew up there. Her grandmother was Violet Cropper, and she had wonderful memories of home and family. She said there was a spirit that she used to talk to when she was little. It was a young man—maybe even an older boy. She would sit on the steps with him, and they'd have discussions. They became friends, and eventually she stopped seeing him. Her mother referred to him as her imaginary friend. But she recalls him being real.

There was an incident involving a young man about eighty years before this woman met her spirit friend on the steps of Tarry-A-While.

The Dennis Hotel was located directly across the street from the Tarry-A-While, and the two families—Dennises and Croppers—were friends. In 1908, Calvin Cropper, the son of Thomas and Sallie, was twenty-one years old. Calvin and Savannah Dennis had been childhood friends, but Calvin fell in love with Savannah as they grew older. Evidently, Savannah didn't take Calvin seriously and dismissed his romantic interests. Calvin became depressed, and his family was worried about him but didn't know how to help. He had mentioned to family members that he wanted to die. No one really knows what happened between Calvin and Savannah. The newspaper reported in Calvin's obituary that he mentioned that he might kill himself to "a young lady, to whom he was paying much attention"—likely Savannah—and the young lady laughed it off.

After the reported conversation, Calvin returned home, walked up the front steps where his mother and brother were sitting and passed them without a word. He entered the house, went to his room and locked the door. Then Calvin lit a cigarette, lay down on his bed, put a gun to his head and pulled the trigger. His mother and brother heard the shot, and his brother had to break down the locked door. He found Calvin on the bed with a cigarette still lit, hanging from his lips, and a gaping gunshot wound in his temple.

The obituary, courtesy of the Ocean City Life-Saving Station Museum, read:

AUGUST 22, 1908 YOUNG MAN KILLS HIMSELF—Calvin T. Cropper 21 years old, son of Thomas J. Cropper, committed suicide at his home late Wednesday night by blowing his brains out with a pistol. Family troubles had been prying on Mr. Cropper's mind for some time, and for a month or more he had threatened to put an end to his life. Wednesday night he went driving with a young lady, to whom he was paying much attention, and who had been a chum of his since school days, and told her he was going to kill himself, but she only laughed at his threat and believed he would soon get over his despondent mood. On the return home Mr. Cropper passed his mother and brother who were sitting on the porch, went to his room and locked the door. A second later a shot was heard and the brother rushed upstairs, broke in the door and found Calvin lying on the bed, pistol in hand, with his coat off and a cigarette in his mouth and blood flowing from his gaping wound in his temple.

Tarry-A-While has been fully restored under the direction of the Ocean City Development Corporation and looks now much as it would have looked back when Thomas and Sallie Cropper first opened it as a guest house a block away from the ocean. Of all the stops on the Ocean City Ghost Walk, Tarry-A-While is the stop where guests get the most anomalies in pictures they take. A recent ghost walk guest picture showed the white, shadowy figure of a man waving from the porch.

The woman I interviewed who grew up in Tarry-A-While recalled stories she heard her grandmother Violet Cropper tell about the time when Calvin died. Violet was Calvin's sister. Violet said that her mother, Sallie, went to visit Calvin's grave every day on horseback. It was eight miles each way and included a ferry crossing. She never got over the tragic loss of her son.

Tarry-A-While has such a mix of energies in and around it. Though it has been moved and renovated, the powerful feelings of love, loss, mourning and closeness of the Cropper family has burned an imprint on the energy field that makes connection with the spirits much easier. The angst of young Calvin, who only saw death as an escape from his emotional pain; the suffering and guilt his parents must have felt; the shock of the suicide; the mourning over the absence of Calvin mixed in with all of the family's happy times—all of this emotion would have had an impact on the energy of the house. The years of Cropper family happiness and the hundred summers of romance and joy that guests experienced while staying at the Tarry-A-While on their vacations surely eclipse any negative or sad energy left behind.

Tarry-A-While still radiates that happy energy—the kind of energy that welcomes humans and spirits alike.

THE PLIM PLAZA

An Ocean City local who is an avid runner said he used to take his early morning run on a stretch of beach that crossed in front of the Plim Plaza Hotel. He noticed that sometimes in the off-season, when the hotel was closed and dark, there would be a light on in one of the upper rooms. He didn't think much of it, as the Harrison Group keeps its offices and headquarters there. On one particular morning, the sun had barely risen; there was a gray, overcast sky, and it was freezing cold. The man slowed his run and crossed the beach in front of the Plim Plaza, moving toward the Boardwalk so as to distance himself from the bitter cold wind coming off the ocean.

He noticed that there was someone walking back and forth across the Plim's oceanfront veranda. As he got closer, it looked like a woman wearing a long skirt but no coat. Everything was closed on that part of the Boardwalk—all the hotels, restaurants and stores. It was so odd to see someone out there that early in the morning. As he ran past the hotel, it occurred to him that maybe she needed help. So he turned back quickly, but she was gone. He figured she must have had access to the hotel.

He saw the woman again that spring. The Boardwalk hotels were still closed, but it was a beautiful morning, and as he ran past the Plim Plaza, he looked up and saw her there. This time, he stopped for a better view. She was wearing the same clothes as before—a long-sleeved white shirt tucked into a long, dark skirt. She was pacing from one end of the veranda to the other like she was waiting for someone or looking for someone. There was no one

The Plim Plaza Hotel, built on the site of the Plinhimmon Hotel.

around—not on the beach and not on the Boardwalk. He thought he might run up there on his way back and ask if she needed anything. But when he came back past the Plim, she was gone.

He never saw her again, and he ran nearly every day. That summer, he was walking on the Boardwalk with friends, and they passed the Plim Plaza. His memory went right back to those two mornings when he saw the woman pacing on the veranda. He was closer to the hotel now, and he noticed that it was impossible to walk from end to end on the veranda because the porch was sectioned off, enclosing private balconies for guest rooms. One would have to hop a few fences in order to walk from one end to the other. It puzzled him. He knew what he saw.

Since those runs, he has never passed this hotel without thinking of her. And now, sitting on a Boardwalk bench in front of the Plim Plaza, he was telling me about her.

It was his story that encouraged me to investigate the Plim Plaza a little further. The management had no stories to tell, but the wait staff at the poolside grill and the elegant Paul Revere restaurant had a few stories to tell. One young woman said that there are "helpers" that help staff in times of their greatest need. A young lady who bussed tables said that when things get too busy, she often gets assistance with menial tasks. Her silverware will be wrapped, napkins folded—things like that. Another said she once forgot to put in an order for a customer who was particularly irritable. When she remembered, she rushed to the kitchen to put the order in, but the order had been placed, and it was prepared and ready to serve. A third server said that she had a customer who had a toddler who kept crying. It was disturbing to the other guests, and the parents were about to leave in frustration. As the server passed the hostess station, there was a brand-new, freshly wrapped lollipop. The hostess said she didn't know where it came from. The server offered it to the parents, who immediately quieted the child with it. The girls I interviewed said everyone figured there was an angel in the house.

The Plim Plaza may or may not have an angel or benevolent spirit that concerns itself with helping the most humble of workers in their greatest times of need. But the hotel surely has great karma. It is connected to two rags-to-riches success stories associated with two prominent Eastern Shore families. It would not be surprising to find it had a lucky angel hanging around.

Rosalie Tilghman Shreve had a great pedigree. She was the daughter of Tench Tilghman, the adjutant general of Maryland. He was a Confederate sympathizer and the owner of the Maryland Delaware Railroad. Her great-grandfather Lieutenant Colonel Tench Tilghman was in General George Washington's Continental army and served as his aide de camp. Rosalie was born in 1846 at Plinhimmon, the Tilghman family plantation in Oxford. The Tilghmans were prosperous and wealthy, according to the standards of the day, and Rosalie lived a privileged life.

During the Civil War, Rosalie fell in love with a man who worked for her father's railroad company. He was from Leesburg, Virginia, and had served in the Confederate army. He was held as a prisoner of war at Fort Delaware. While in prison, he developed tuberculosis, and he was granted a release with the understanding that he would not return to Virginia. His name was Thomas Shreve, and he and Rosalie married in 1865, when Rosalie was nineteen years old. Within a year, their first son, Oswald, was born, followed by Arthur in 1868.

When the war ended, Rosalie's father found himself on the losing side. All of his slaves had to be released, his railroad failed and he went bankrupt. Shortly after Arthur was born, Thomas Shreve finally succumbed to his illness. Rosalie was left at age twenty-one with two children to support and no family to lean on in a country that was in economic chaos. She left Plinhimmon and moved to Baltimore with her two small boys and made her way in the world by running a rooming house. Around 1890, Rosalie began renting Goldsborough Cottage in Ocean City and running it as a guest house every summer. She managed to save enough money to buy two oceanfront building lots at the Boardwalk and Third Street. Then she financed the building of a forty-eight-room Victorian hotel, designed with all the modern conveniences of the day, including electric lights, electric call bells and sanitary plumbing. She was fifty years old, and in 1890, she was doing something no woman had ever done in Ocean City.

Rosalie named her new hotel the Plinhimmon after her beloved childhood home. She was successful beyond her wildest dreams and became one of the richest women in Ocean City. She ran the hotel until her death in 1920, and her family continued to run it for years after that. Forty-two years after Rosalie died, the seventy-two-year-old Plinhimmon Hotel caught fire and burned to the ground. It was the end of a beautiful story. The hotel was rebuilt in a more modern style, and the builders placed a Victorian tower on top—similar to the Plinhimmon's tower—in order to link the new hotel with the memory of the Plinhimmon.

The hotel was renamed the Plim Plaza. It was time for a new success story.

Orlando Harrison of Berlin led the Harrison Brothers Nurseries to becoming the largest producer of fruit trees and ornamental shrubs in the

The Plinhimmon Hotel, built by Rosalie Tilghman, burned to the ground in 1962. Postcard view.

world. It employed between 250 and 500 workers in its operation, and Orlando, who became a Maryland state senator, paid out more money in wages than any other man in Worcester County for forty straight years. When Orlando died, his son G. Hale Harrison was running the nursery operation. At age forty-nine, G. Hale fell in love with and married a woman named Lois, whom he met on a blind date at the Shoreham Hotel in Ocean City (the most haunted property in Ocean City). Lois was in the hotel business and had just been named the new manager at the Shoreham. In the 1950s, while still managing the Harrison Brothers Nurseries, G. Hale built a hotel in Ocean City and called it Harrison Hall. It was a gift for his wife.

In the early 1960s, a peach blight wiped out most of the Harrison orchards. They lost most of their farms, and the business folded, but G. Hale and his wife continued with their hotel operation. In 1961, G. Hale died, leaving Lois with three young children. Their eldest, Hale, was only thirteen years old. If losing her husband after the nursery failure wasn't enough, Lois and the children faced the devastating storm of 1962 the year after they lost G. Hale. In a video interview, Hale Harrison states that times were rough financially. But they got through it, bounced back, and his mother continued to grow the Harrison Hall hotel business. Lois became ill when Hale was in college, and he left school to help her with the hotel business. Within a year, he and his brother John put a down payment on the Plim Plaza Hotel. Hale was twenty-two, and John was twenty-one. The brothers eventually formed the Harrison Group, which today owns ten oceanfront resort hotels and twelve restaurants—all in Ocean City. Their offices and headquarters are located at the Plim Plaza Hotel. The Harrison Group is one of the largest property owners and private employers in Worcester County.

So this unique property, this yellow oceanfront hotel with a Victorian tower built as a memorial to the Plinhimmon, has two family legacies attached to it in which both families faced what must have seemed like insurmountable obstacles and then rose above them to be more successful than they'd ever imagined. In its own way, the Plim Plaza is a reminder to all entrepreneurs who fail, fall on bad times or find challenges they think they'll never overcome that dreams still can come true. The Plim Plaza has good karma. It's no wonder there are helping angels all around.

As for the lady who walks the veranda in a long skirt—who knows? It wouldn't surprise me if Rosalie Tilghman Shreve were beginning her day with her favorite view of the ocean. Spirits often alight where they found the most joy in life. While she found her first joy at Plinhimmon, her childhood home in Oxford, she discovered her place of resurrection where her spirit was most at home at the Plinhimmon Hotel in Ocean City. That block at Third Street and the Boardwalk will always belong to Rosalie.

The Tilghmans are a family of famous ghosts. Several family members are believed to haunt different places on the Eastern Shore. Rosalie's brother Colonel Oswald Tilghman is said to haunt both the Talbot County Courthouse and his Easton home, known as Foxley Hall—reportedly the most haunted house in Easton. Lieutenant Colonel Tench Tilghman, Rosalie's great-grandfather, rode nonstop from Yorktown to Philadelphia on horseback carrying the message of the British surrender to the Continental Congress. His ghost has been seen riding on the part of that old road that crosses Chestertown near the bridge at St. Paul's Cemetery. His widow, Anna Marie Tilghman, is believed to haunt the old Plinhimmon plantation, which survives in pristine condition in Oxford on a piece of land that overlooks the Oxford cemetery and the Tilghman graves.

RANDY HOFMAN SAND SCULPTURES

The sand sculptures along the Boardwalk opposite the Plim Plaza are worth mentioning here because they are rooted in spirituality. Years ago, when someone asked Randy Hofman why he started doing these religious sand sculptures, he replied that Jesus told him to. He continually comments that he sees his life's purpose as relaying the words of Jesus in art.

Hofman is a sixty-two-year-old painter and sand sculptor. He is also an ordained minster. He's been sculpting biblical scenes in front of the Plim Plaza for over twenty years. No one pays him to do it. There is a donation jar for those who feel inclined to give and a jar with scripture-inscribed pamphlets that are free for the taking.

Anyone who walks the Boardwalk between Second and Third Streets in the summer months will see a small (or large) crowd stopped in front of Hofman's amazing creations. Some of his sculptures are ten feet high and forty feet wide. His only tools are a spade, a knife, water and his hands. He also uses a little spray bottle of watered-down glue that makes a protective crust that holds up against a gentle rain or wind. Since he started the sculptures twenty years ago, he's distributed over one million of his free scripture pamphlets.

Hofman explains that the sand sculptures are like human bodies. Nature keeps trying to break them down, to erode the surface, to wash them away

Last Supper, sand sculpture by artist Randy Hofman.

Randy Hofman has been doing sand sculptures near the Boardwalk at Third Street for twenty years.

and return the sculptures back to the sand where they came from. He advises us to book our reservations in advance because we'll never know when a wave will come in with our name on it.

The Plim Plaza provides the water Hofman needs to create the sculptures. It also provides the electric lights that light up the sculptures at night. One can't pass by these works of art and not be moved to take a few steps into the spirit world. The sculptures mesh well with the positive energy that vibrates around the Plim Plaza.

WHO IS BURIED AT CAPTAIN'S HILL?

E very one of our Chesapeake Ghost Walks includes a walk through a graveyard—except Ocean City. In Ocean City, there are no graveyards, no cemeteries. There is but one lone marked grave, and not only is it the only marked grave in Ocean City, but it is also the only known grave in the area of a shipwreck victim.

In West Ocean City, in a residential development known as Captain's Hill, there is a four-foot-tall marble headstone with a matching footstone that sits in the corner of someone's yard (granted, it is a large front lawn). Along with the headstone and footstone is a giant ship's anchor, which tips the visitor off that this is a memorial of some kind.

It is a memorial to a sea captain named William Carhart, who was thirty-eight years old in 1798 when he steered his ship, the *Hawk*, out of his homeport in Philadelphia and arrived in Cuba that December. He sailed out of Cuba bound for home on Christmas Day, likely carrying a large cargo of sugar. On the eleventh day of Christmas, the Eve of the Epiphany, the *Hawk* sank off the coast of Ocean City near the Sinepuxent Inlet. The ship and crew were lost.

The headstone reads:

In Memory of
Capt. William Carhart
Shipwrecked off this coast
January 5, 1799
Aged 38 years and 5 months

Captain's Hill in West Ocean City. The grave of Captain William Carhart, who died in 1799.

Up until 1991, most people had no idea who Captain Carhart was. It was a mystery. There were so many questions. Who was the captain? Where was he from (Carhart is not a local name)? What ship was he on? Who put the marker there? Who buried him? Where is his crew?

There were several legends that surfaced, but most were full of inaccuracies because there wasn't much to go on. The people who buried Captain Carhart in this place didn't leave any information behind about who they were. It's likely that they weren't from the area. But the research of Joan D. Charles of Hampton, Virginia, brought us some clarity. It was she who found the information on Captain Carhart's origins, his destination, the name of his ship, what kind of cargo he was carrying and the fact that both ship and crew were lost.

Research shows that January 1799 was a particularly cold month—the coldest anyone at the time remembered. It's likely that Captain Carhart and his crew died from exposure to the elements. No one could last long in water temperatures that cold. Charles's research also uncovered that Captain Carhart had a wife in Philadelphia, and it was she who ordered and paid for the marker. Marble commanded a hefty price in 1799, as did transporting it to Ocean City, and it's because the memorial is made of marble that it has withstood the toll that salt air and coastal storms take on grave markers.

We still don't know what happened to the crew or who buried Captain Carhart, but a local mariner named Captain Jack Bunting said that a cow once stepped in what looked like a grave near where Captain Carhart is buried. Perhaps his crew is buried nearby, but no markers were afforded them because there was no one who could bear that expense. We may never know.

On Graves and Graveyards

I was very curious about why there were no graveyards in Ocean City when I started to do my research for the ghost walks and this book. When I posed the question to people, the common response was that the water table was too high, and graves would be washed away over time. Possible, but unlikely. There are graveyards in Hooper's Island, Deal Island and Assateague Island. Rehoboth and Lewes also have plenty of cemeteries. The low-lying areas may have used concrete or brick vaults to secure caskets, but they had to bury their dead no matter how high the water table was. When families couldn't access communal graveyards like church graveyards, they would open up private family cemeteries on their land. Graveyards are all over the Eastern Shore, and they existed in every community. And if you can build a fifteen- to twenty-story hotel on the ground in Ocean City, you can surely bury a few bodies.

Another explanation for not having graveyards was not wanting to compromise land in such a highly coveted real estate market. This also made no sense because there was plenty of space in Ocean City's early years. Small towns everywhere followed the same process. Communities gathered around churches, and when people died, the churches handled the funerals and burials. The most likely place for a graveyard—at least in the late nineteenth and early twentieth centuries—was the church. But the prominent families in Ocean City—the Croppers, the Lynches, the Trimpers, the Purnells—they were all buried in Berlin.

What is the difference between a graveyard and a cemetery? A graveyard is in the yard of a church, and a cemetery is a piece of land set aside for burials typically with no affiliation to a church or denomination. The first church built in Ocean City was St. Mary's Star of the Sea on Baltimore

Avenue at Talbot Street. It is also the oldest existing building in Ocean City, erected in 1878, just three years after Ocean City was founded. It has a rectory beside the church building but no graveyard. The way the church is positioned on the lot seems to indicate that the builders never intended for a graveyard to be there. And there was plenty of space for a graveyard in 1878.

It was historian George Hurley who suggested to me that there were no plans for a graveyard at St. Mary's because the Catholic church was built for nonresidents. He explained that the owners of the Atlantic Hotel petitioned the bishop of the Wilmington Diocese to put a church near the hotel so their seasonal workers (who were predominantly Catholic) could go to Sunday Mass. The same bishop of Wilmington was also interested in building a facility where priests from the diocese could go on retreat. So there were no permanent residents using that church. The notion that there were no graveyards or family cemeteries in Ocean City because the year-round population was so sparse made sense.

But what about the people who did die in Ocean City? What if there was a death in February when the weather was frigid? How would the family transport the deceased to Berlin when it required a ferry ride and an eight-mile trip in the freezing cold by horse and buggy? How could a funeral and burial be pulled together in a timely way considering there was a dead body subject to decomposition that had to be transported out of the community?

Kirk Burbage, owner of Burbage Funeral Homes, answered these questions for me. Burbage's is the oldest continually operating funeral home in Maryland, having been founded in 1810. It's Kirk's ancestors who would have dealt with Ocean City deaths in the late nineteenth century. Kirk explained that embalming became common practice during the Civil War because, with so many battlefield deaths, the time frame for getting the remains of deceased soldiers back to their people was sometimes months. Embalming in those days was done mostly with pure formaldehyde, which could preserve a body for a very long time. Today, due to the carcinogenic nature of formaldehyde, the pure form is no longer used. Kirk said his great-grandparents would travel to Ocean City when someone had died, and they would embalm the deceased on-site and assist with the funeral or memorial service there in the home. Then, after all the family members and friends had the opportunity to pay their respects, the Burbages would transport the body back to Berlin for burial.

Mystery solved. There are no graveyards or cemeteries in Ocean City because there was never enough of a core population to warrant one.

Embalming and funeral services were available in the home from a Berlin undertaker who would then transport the preserved body back to Berlin for burial. When the population finally grew large enough that it could support a cemetery, the real estate was too precious, and Berlin was only a ten-minute drive away.

It is stories like the one about Captain Carhart and his crew that reveal how important graveyards and memorials are to the living. In a day when so many dismiss burials, funerals and memorial services as unneeded expenses, we're slowly becoming a nation that looks at the death process through a sterilized screen. We think that if we view death as unpleasant—something we shouldn't dwell on—then we'll suffer less. If we don't face death in its raw form—look at the face of the deceased, touch his hand, cry at his graveside and memorialize him in stone—then we won't hurt so much. If we don't focus on it, then we can't be sad. This attitude just prolongs the grieving process and dishonors the loved one who has passed away.

Remembering is an act of love, and a grave marker is a manifestation of that love. The dead don't care. These memorials are for the living. How moving it is to walk through the old graveyards and see how people memorialized loved ones fifty years ago, one hundred years ago, two hundred years ago. A lily marking the grave of a teenage daughter who died too soon, a weeping willow on the tombstone of a beloved father, a little chair with tiny shoes atop the grave of an infant—every marker tells a story, every story is linked to what people remember and the memory is joined to the spirit that has passed. And though there is sorrow to bear when those left behind erect these markers, in time, that sorrow eases, and a grave becomes a peaceful place of connection and remembrance.

It is good to remember that people lived and people loved, and that living and loving matter. Grave markers proclaim this and offer subtle reminders of this truth to those who pass by even centuries later.

I visited my grandfather's grave a few years ago, and the comfort I got from tracing my fingers along his name on the marker was indescribable. All at once, all of my memories of him swirled around me, and I was overwhelmed. It was a physical act that brought on a spiritual connection.

I so hope my generation will reconsider not binding their loved ones with stringent instructions on how to handle their bodies after death. Naturally, we don't want to saddle a surviving family with unbearable expense, but it's the survivors who benefit, the survivors who mark the moment with meaning, the survivors who need to let go and move forward. Just as traveling every day to the grave of her son Calvin helped Sallie Cropper, erecting a marble memorial on her husband's grave helped William Carhart's wife and tracing my grandfather's name on his headstone helped me, grave markers serve an important purpose. They tell a story. They connect the living with their ancestors. They help the sorrowful to heal.

DOLLE'S CANDYLAND

In 1906, Rudolph Dolle, a Brooklyn, New York carousel dealer, and his thirteen-year-old son, Rudolph W., came to Ocean City at the invitation of Daniel Trimper. The Dolles designed and manufactured hand-carved carousels in the Coney Island style. Daniel Trimper was hoping to expand the amusements near the Pier to meet the growing demand from tourists. The Dolles moved to Ocean City soon after that and set up a carousel at the Boardwalk and Wicomico Street, where Dolle's Candy is located today.

In 1910, a man who made salt water taffy on a cart near the Dolles' carousel operation intrigued Rudolph Dolle. In the early 1880s, salt water taffy was created by accident in Atlantic City. A candy store owner named David Bradley experienced a flood during an Atlantic storm. His entire stock of taffy was ruined, covered in ocean water. While he was cleaning up the mess, a little girl came in and asked if he had any taffy. He joked and said he had some "salt water taffy." He gave the little girl some of the taffy, and it turned out that she loved it. She told her friends and brought more kids to the store to buy this salt water taffy. After awhile, the name stuck, and though salt water taffy doesn't (and never has) contain seawater, it does contain both salt and water.

To make the salt water taffy on the cart, the man had to cook the taffy in a copper kettle, cool it on a marble slab and then pull it by hand on a large hook. Atlantic City candy dealers branded salt water taffy as a souvenir for tourists and packaged it in various sizes. Rudolph Dolle loved the idea of making candy, and he bought the man's cart and his taffy operation.

Left: Rudolph Dolle Sr. with son Rudolph in 1906, taken on the Ocean City Pier. *Image courtesy of Anna Dolle Bushnell.*

Right: Rudolph W. Dolle kept this photo of his father, Rudolph Sr., in his wallet since the day they arrived in Ocean City. *Image courtesy of Anna Dolle Bushnell.*

Rudolph died in 1916, but Rudolph W. took the lead in the family business, and the Dolles continued to make taffy. They found that taffy and the carousel business went together well.

But 1925 was the year of the Great Boardwalk Fire. It began at the electric company on Somerset Street and Baltimore Avenue and ended up destroying three square blocks, including the Atlantic Hotel, the Pier, the Casino Theater, several other hotels and the Dolles' operation. The fire destroyed the Dolles' beautiful hand-carved carousel. So Rudolph W. decided to focus on candy. He expanded the business to include caramel popcorn and caramel candy. Later, he added fudge. He developed a manufacturing operation right on Wicomico Street behind the candy storefront. He named the business Dolle's Candyland.

Rudolph W. was an entrepreneurial spirit and continued to grow the Dolle's Candyland operation until his death in 1968. After his death, his daughter Evelyn ran the company until her death in 1978, when the company passed to Rudolph W. Jr. Today, Rudolph W. Jr.'s children, Anna and Andrew, run

A 1920s view of Dolle's Candyland on the Boardwalk. *Image courtesy of Anna Dolle Bushnell.*

the company, which still operates out of that same location at the Boardwalk and Wicomico Street.

As the fourth generation leads the company, the candy is still manufactured daily in the facility behind the store. Dolle's employs about fifty people and has four locations. It manufactures caramels, fudge, truffles, gummy candies, licorice, homemade specialty candies, caramel popcorn—and, yes, Dolle's still makes its famous salt water taffy. All of Dolle's candy is made fresh every day with love.

But Dolle's Candyland has a few ghosts hanging around the Wicomico Street location. It once had an employee who worked there for over fifty years. Her name was Katherine, and she befriended Rudolph W. when she arrived in Ocean City from her home in Philadelphia. Katherine's early life is unknown, but she admitted that she felt the need to leave Philly, so she snuck into the trunk of a car and figured she'd get out wherever it stopped and make a new life. It stopped at the Boardwalk in Ocean City.

Katherine lived at the store for a while and worked as a manager in the candy store. She was spunky and opinionated but well loved by the Dolle's employees and family. Katherine died in 1999. Employees who have worked at Dolle's for over twenty years remember Katherine. One recalls that

Katherine sold Avon products and wore a very strong perfume. The same employee has sensed Katherine's presence in the store and smelled her strong perfume. Anna Dolle Bushnell says she believes Katherine is present and likes to create a little mischief here and there—hiding things and knocking things over.

Anna carries a big ball of keys around with her, and she admits that they are easy to find due to the size of the key cluster. But she's lost

Left: Dolle's Candies always combines the old with the new in its packaging. The stars on the candy wrapping are from Dolle's original 1920s design.

Below: Rudolph W. Dolle and his wife, Vashti. *Image courtesy of Anna Dolle Bushnell.*

them on occasion and will look frantically and then finally call out, "Katherine, give me my keys back!" Then the keys will show up in some unexpected place. There was also an incident where a manager went into the manufacturing facility to get taffy to take to another store. He discovered taffy all over the floor, and it had to be discarded. No one could understand how the taffy got there. The management checked the video footage from the security cameras and saw a twenty-pound tub of taffy flip itself over, spilling taffy onto the floor. There was no trace of any human being in the facility at the time.

Anna also feels a close affinity with the spirit of her grandfather Rudolph W. She senses his benevolent presence leading and guiding her in the Wicomico Street facility. From time to time, she says he gives her advice. Internally, she can hear his voice. It was he who advised her to incorporate some of the old with the new when she was reviewing graphic designs for candy packaging, which is why she chose little stars that appear on the ends of the wrapped candies. Those stars were part of the original Dolle's candy packaging.

Her grandfather will also prod her to go home when she's working late and encourage her when she's overwhelmed. Anna senses his protective energy all around the store and the Dolle family.

THE DUNES MANOR HOTEL

Thelma Conner is a legend in Ocean City. Like Rosalie Tilghman Shreve, Thelma pioneered a dream that everyone around her said was too grand to come true. Thelma joined her husband, Milton, in the hotel business shortly after they were married. His mother owned the Hastings Hotel, and that's where a lifetime of welcoming and hospitality began for Thelma Conner. In 1963, when the motel craze started in America, Thelma and Milton opened the Dunes Motel at Twenty-seventh Street at the northern end of the Boardwalk.

They were very successful, and Thelma treated her staff, as well as her guests, like family. She knew that if you could get a group of people to interact with one another, they would have a better time, and Thelma was a master at engaging people. It wasn't unusual for her to pick up a few Dunes Motel staff members in her car and bring them to work in the morning. She was a strong woman with a big heart. She and Milton dreamed of building a full-service Victorian hotel where tea was served in the afternoons and guests could come together in a welcoming lobby or relax on porches with water views.

Sadly, Milton died before their dream came true, but Thelma pressed on, even though she was getting up in years. When most recently widowed women of her age were thinking about getting rid of things and slowing down, Thelma was making plans to build an eleven-story, Victorian-style, full-service hotel. She would build next door to the Dunes Motel on land she had inherited. Everyone said she was a fool to start something so large

The Dunes Manor Hotel, built by Thelma Conner when she was seventy-five years old. It was opened on April Fool's Day because people said Thelma was a fool for building it.

when she was so old. So, as a response to those remarks, Thelma had the grand opening of the Dunes Manor Hotel on April Fool's Day 1989. She was seventy-five years old.

Miss Thelma added some special touches to the new hotel. She always believed that people were happiest when they were interacting with other people, so the Dunes Manor served afternoon tea every day at 3:00 p.m., and Miss Thelma would often do the pouring. In the evening, there was a sing-along in the lobby around a grand piano. There were rockers on the verandas, a formal restaurant overlooking the ocean and a casual lounge Thelma named after the famous widowed beachcomber Zippy Lewis.

The lobby is furnished with antiques, and there are framed images of old Ocean City hanging throughout the hotel. The public spaces are welcoming and relaxing, just as Miss Thelma designed them. The traditions of sing-alongs around the piano and afternoon tea continue today. Hotel staff will often reminisce about how Miss Thelma would show up in the lobby to serve her guests afternoon tea. Most of the time, the guests had no idea that the sweet old lady pouring their tea and chatting with them about their stay was the owner of the hotel. Thelma simply wanted her guests to feel like family, and the afternoon tea tradition helped bring that kind of welcome to Dunes Manor Hotel guests.

Miss Thelma passed away in 1999, and the hotel was left to family members. It is still a family-owned hotel. Large painted portraits of Thelma and Milton Conner hang in prominent positions in the two-story lobby at the Dunes Manor Hotel. No one can get to the front desk without passing the portraits, which have a dominating presence. And there is a general feeling of acceptance among most of the hotel staff that Miss Thelma is still around.

Guests and staff alike pass by Miss Thelma's portrait and speak. They might say, "Good morning, Miss Thelma," or "Goodnight, Miss Thelma," or "What do you think of this, Miss Thelma?" Talking to the portrait seems natural. That kind yet demanding

Portrait of Thelma Connor, founder of the Dunes Manor Hotel. *Courtesy of the Dunes Manor Hotel.*

face in the oil painting begs to be recognized. Several staff members admit that sometimes Miss Thelma answers back. After adding new lamps to the front desk, the hotel's general manager—in front of the front desk staff—turned to the portrait and said, "Thelma, what do you think of the new lamps?" Instantly, recessed lights on the vaulted ceiling above the portrait flashed. No one at the hotel could remember those lights ever working. At the time, they couldn't even figure out where the on/off switch was.

There's also a light in the lobby known to blink when guests and staff reach out verbally to Miss Thelma, and the restaurant manager, who has been a Dunes Manor employee since the hotel's opening, says that there is a rocker that acts up on the veranda outside the restaurant. She says that when the wind blows and all the rockers start rocking, there is always one lone rocker that sits perfectly still as if someone is holding it in place. The restaurant manager believes it's the spirit of Milton Conner. He would have liked that view.

A guest posted a review on TripAdvisor entitled "Nice Stay but Haunted." According to the reviewer, her family stayed at the Dunes Manor for three nights. They loved their room and the service, but the reviewer's fourteen-year-old son woke his mother up when he saw an old lady walk across their room and go through the balcony door. His mother wrote:

> *The weird thing that happened was around 12:30 a.m. the last night we were there. My 14-year-old son woke me up to say he had seen an old lady walk across the room and go through the balcony door. He was wide-awake when this happened as he was playing a game on his phone. He described her to me and I had him Google a picture of Thelma Conner, the former owner who had since passed away. Sure enough it was her…So if you happen to stay in room 608 you may be able to say hello to the founder of the hotel.*

Thelma Conner's portrait on the wall of the lobby stairway does command the visitors' attention. Recently, vandals came into the Dunes Manor early one Sunday morning, probably about 3:00 a.m. They somehow managed to climb up high enough to snag Miss Thelma's portrait and make off with it. When the staff came in the next morning, Thelma was gone. It was a shock, not just because a pair of hooligans had managed to pull it off, but also because that guardian presence that had been watching over them seemed absent. Two days later, the portrait was found at the EconoLodge next door to the Dunes Manor. A maid had found it in one of the rooms. So Miss Thelma returned to her proper place less than three days after she went on an adventure with a couple of thieves.

One can only wonder how they slept that night with Miss Thelma's eye on them.

THE LEGEND OF ZIPPY LEWIS

The Dunes Manor Hotel has a lounge named in honor of Ocean City's famed beachcomber Zippy Lewis. Located directly across from the Dunes Manor's Victorian Room by the Sea, the Zippy Lewis Lounge is a more casual setting. The lounge is snug and familiar, and an oil painting of a woman dressed in a long bonnet and apron walking out of the marsh onto the beach is a focal point in the lounge. Artist David Bunting created the painting, and it has all the colors one would expect on a sunny day at the seashore. The style is similar to that of American impressionist Frank

Artist David O. Bunting's rendering of Zippy Lewis hangs in the Dunes Manor lounge named in her memory.

Benson, who painted all of those Victorian ladies by the shore. But the detail in the face of Bunting's lady with the apron is clear and deep, similar to the faces of the mothers Mary Cassatt painted.

The lady in Bunting's painting is Zipporah "Zippy" Lewis, a legendary widow who lived in a shack in north Ocean City back when the area was wooded. She was from Delaware. She married Jonathan Lewis at age sixteen and had her first child—a son, Jacob—in 1829. The three of them settled on the beach around 1830. Jonathan was a fisherman. They built a life there and had four more children. Shortly after their fifth child was born, Jonathan Lewis went to sea. Weeks passed, and Zippy began to walk the dunes looking out to sea, trying to spot her husband's ship. Every day she walked the dunes, anticipating his return.

He never came back.

Zippy was left a widow with five children in 1847. She had no means of support except for what she could scrounge off the beach and sell in town. So she and her children would comb the beach for coins, debris and odd junk washed up from shipwrecks and vessels lost at sea. Bunting's painting shows Zippy in a blue linsey-woolsey dress, which was made from a fabric that was a combination of wool and linen. Because of the fabric's durability and warmth, and because it was relatively cheap, it was worn by people who couldn't afford much better. Slaves and orphans were commonly clad in linsey-woolsey. Zippy's white apron would have been used for gathering the items she collected, but in the painting, Zippy is also carrying a basket. Her soft brown eyes, shaded by the brim of her corded bonnet, are clear and sad. Her gaze is pensive. She is focused on the sea.

There is a little framed sign hanging next to the painting that reads:

ZIPPY LEWIS LOUNGE
Zipporah "Zippy" Lewis is one of Ocean City's more colorful characters from the past. Zipporah's husband, a sailor, was lost at sea shortly before the Civil War began. Awaiting his return, which was never to be, Mrs. Lewis became a lonely recluse taking residence in a shack that she built in north Ocean City where it is believed that she raised wild cattle. Legend has it that "Aunt Zippy" lived by foraging the beach, even replenishing her supplies and foodstuffs from the flotsam of shipwrecks. During the 1820s a ship laden with coins foundered in a storm off of the coast of Ocean City. For many years after, Nor'easter storms would wash the coins up on the beach. It is said that Zipporah collected them and could be seen driving her ox-cart between Berlin and

Bishopville, where she visited the stores and exchanged the coins and cattle for merchandise. Her legend lives on at the Dunes Manor in the Zippy Lewis Lounge.

Legends are contrived when little bits and pieces of dangling truths are woven together to make a logical story. People fill in the gaps with something that sounds embellished, and after a while, the legend is far from the actual truth. I think this is probably the case with Zippy Lewis.

We know that Zippy Lewis lived on land that is near where the Carousel Hotel is located today. In 1856, she acquired seventy acres of land, and it was issued in her name only. By this time, her husband would have been dead for about ten years. It's likely that Zippy was already living on that land and was living in a house made from reused junk that had washed up on the beach and some timbers that were on her land. Wealthy farmers who used the land to graze cattle formerly owned the land Zippy acquired. It's likely that a great storm in the early 1800s flooded the land and made it undesirable for grazing. The owners stopped paying taxes, the land was forfeited and the local government reissued patents. When Zippy got her patents, her three sons were in their twenties. She was still supporting her two daughters.

The legends also tell of Zippy polling her boat across Assawoman Bay to the mainland and riding from Bishopville to Berlin in her oxcart, selling her found wares to stores and merchants. Such was the way Zippy provided for her family. It was a tough life.

Zippy's story usually ends when the storyteller says that her house burned down with her in it. Sometimes that story states that she threw herself into the fire, and then the fire consumed the house. The house did burn but not until well after Zippy's death in 1879. It's likely that Zippy fell into the fireplace in her house and was burned badly, and that injury eventually led to her death. Some of Zippy's descendants say that she died of consumption. Zippy is most likely buried at Mount Zion Cemetery in Bayard, Delaware. There is no marker for her, but most of her children, including her two daughters, Gincy and Mary, are buried there.

Zippy, in her will, left a few dollars each to her two living sons and a few dollars to her son Jacob's descendants (Jacob died at sea). But she left her land and her house to her two daughters, who were both grown with families. It's likely that the lighthouse keepers at the Fenwick Island Lighthouse are the ones who saw Zippy combing the beach. Theirs was a bird's-eye view, and they would be able to scour the land readily. Zippy had almost no neighbors.

Zipporah Lewis's story is a tribute to women—especially women who face what seem to be insurmountable challenges. Zippy pushed on, as did Rosalie Shreve, Thelma Conner and so many other women who were the drive and foundation of Ocean City as it grew over the years.

Some say that on moonlit nights you can still see Zippy Lewis walking the beach and the dunes or polling her boat across Assawoman Bay. Others say that if you find a coin on the beach, Zippy probably dropped it, hoping you'd find it. She's on the beach, she's in the dunes, she's driving an oxcart and crossing the Bay and she is living in the memories of many Ocean City and Delaware locals.

THE SHOREHAM HOTEL

In the early 1920s, Josephine Hastings built the Shoreham Hotel at the Boardwalk and Fourth Street. Today, it's one of the oldest hotels in Ocean City. It was built on pilings instead of a concrete block foundation and could withstand the storms and tidal surges that destroyed other hotels. During the Ash Wednesday storm in 1962, many of the small hotels on the ocean were simply washed away—knocked off their foundations by the surging tides. But the Shoreham stood firm and is still standing strong today.

The Shoreham is also the place where G. Hale Harrison of Harrison Brothers Nurseries met his beloved wife, Lois Carmean. The North Carolina management company that was contracted to manage the Shoreham Hotel hired Lois as the hotel manager. G. Hale's sister-in-law, Nadine, set him up with Lois on a blind date. They fell in love quickly, married months later and had sons who would grow up to create the Harrison Hotel Group in Ocean City. The Shoreham has good karma.

It is also probably the most haunted place in historic Ocean City.

The Shoreham Hotel is the site of a suicide, a murder and an accidental death. If human emotion has an impact on an energy field and makes the veil thin between the two worlds, then certainly an accidental death would affect the field, as would a suicide. Top those two off with a murder, and you have the haunted trifecta. There are bound to be spirits around.

According to the Shoreham's owner, Greg Shockley, there's a happy ghost, a sad ghost and a bad ghost. Greg said that a writer staying at the hotel in the 1930s hanged himself in one of the Oceanside rooms on the second floor.

The Shoreham Hotel in Ocean City was the site of a murder, a suicide and an accidental death.

No one knows for sure which room, but there is ghostly activity on that floor. The writer is the sad ghost.

In the 1980s, a twenty-three-year-old local girl named Betsey was staying in Room 6 on the top floor, which is reserved for seasonal housing or guests like students and young people with seasonal jobs who stay for the entire summer. According to staff at the Shoreham, Betsey was a sweet girl. Everyone liked her. One night, she had a little too much to drink, and embracing a fun challenge as young, inebriated people often do, Betsey decided to step out of her fourth-floor window and walk on the ledge from room to room saying hi to all of her friends. Sadly, she slipped and fell to her death on the pavement below. Betsey is the happy ghost.

In 1983, the Shoreham had a bar in the basement known as the Surf and Suds Lounge. A young man from Florida had just finished training as a U.S. Army Green Beret. He was in Ocean City with his friend, who was from Baltimore. They went into the Surf and Suds Lounge and had a few drinks. According to the Green Beret's memoir, a very drunk and belligerent patron taunted him and tried to start a fight. He described the man as being taller and heavier than himself and acting like he was hyped up on a controlled substance such as cocaine. The Green Beret said the man's movements were wild and jerky and that his demeanor was violent and intimidating. The newspaper quoted an eyewitness as saying the man was crazed.

Because of his Green Beret training, he feared having a confrontation with the man. He thought he might kill him. He says that he resisted the taunts of the drunken guy and even left at one point. But the enraged drunken man continued to taunt him. Finally, the drunk cornered the Green Beret at the bar, and a fight broke out. The Green Beret struck the drunken man in the face with a blow that ended up killing him. Police investigated the incident as a murder, and the case was turned over to the Worcester County state's attorney, who brought it before a grand jury. The grand jury did not indict and remarked that the Green Beret's hands were not deadly weapons.

Folks at the Shoreham think that the spirit of that crazed man is haunting the basement, which is no longer a bar. He is the bad ghost.

Staff at the Shoreham have observed unexplained events, weird sounds, strange feelings and odd occurrences in all parts of the hotel. But the basement, which is now a storage area, is a place that Shoreham Hotel staff fear. Very few workers will go down there. Some of them have shared stories about being touched, hearing their names called out in an eerie way, seeing things fly off the shelves and having lights go out or flicker. Several employees have said that they felt a rush of cold air go by them when they went into the basement to retrieve supplies. Greg Shockley said, "I have people who work for me who are terrified to go in there."

But Room 6 on the top floor, where Betsey stayed, is a happy place. The Shoreham Hotel manager says that Room 6 always seems to stay clean. She said that the seasonal rooms are generally rented out by students or young people, and typically that age group is a messy bunch. But whoever stays in Betsey's old room always leaves it immaculate. Almost no deep cleaning has to be done. Room 6 also seems to have more than its share of electronic problems. The television stops working, lights flicker or the volume on the television will arbitrarily increase and decrease with no one touching the controls.

Guests have heard voices on the second floor—particularly children's. One particular guest claimed he heard kids talking about a telephone or talking on the telephone. He couldn't see them, though, and there was no phone in the hall. But the Shoreham staff stated that, years back, there was a telephone in that area. It's long since gone, but there was one located where the guest heard what he thought were guests talking on the phone.

The Blue Mountain Paranormal Society from northeastern Pennsylvania did an investigation at the Shoreham Hotel and found many unexplained phenomena. According to the Shoreham Hotel staff, Blue Mountain set up cameras on the top floor (Betsey's floor) and shut off all things that were electronic on the floor—lights, televisions, clocks, etc.—so as not to have any foreign electromagnetic energy flowing into the environment. All the guest room doors were open, and the investigators set up a camera in the hallway. Room 6 appeared to glow in the photos. Something in the room was emitting enough soft light that it penetrated the doorway, and the "glow" showed up on camera. Other strange things occurred in Room 6 and showed up on the video camera the group planted in the room. The television came on by itself, and then it would go off again. They could also see cloudy spots that almost looked like soap suds circling around the room.

Then Blue Mountain picked up voices on an electronic voice phenomena recorder when investigators asked the spirits questions. One recorded message was, "Mark is going to be pissed." When Blue Mountain members played the recording for Shoreham staff and asked if there was a Mark working there, they were both surprised and amazed. There was a former employee named Mark who had left the Shoreham months before. They said he was very protective of the hotel and all goings on, and had he still been there, he most likely would have objected to the investigation.

A man on the investigation team who had years of experience doing investigations shut himself in the Shoreham basement in order to investigate the presence of the so-called bad ghost. The Shoreham staff was startled when the investigator began to have what seemed like an emotional breakdown in the basement. He evidently couldn't get the door open and began yelling to get him out of there. He later told the rest of his team that he felt unsafe. The ghost came up to him, and he felt a rush of cold air. He could feel the ghost. He broke out in a sweat. He said the presence of that ghost was dark, foreboding and evil. He also said that nothing like that had ever happened to him, and he'd never felt so scared in an investigation.

The investigators found activity in Rooms 215 and 218. They set up cameras in those rooms, and the televisions came on by themselves. In one room, they cut off again. In the other room, the television stayed on and the volume increased and decreased on its own. They also heard knocks on the doors. The investigators also picked up the sounds of children on the first floor. They were laughing and happy. The investigators also saw shadows move on the first floor near where they heard the children.

On the first ghost walk I ever led in Ocean City, I had about fifteen guests. Toward the end of the tour, the skies broke open, and it poured rain. I have never been so drenched. The guests stuck with me and got to the Shoreham, which was the end of the tour. I took the guests inside the hotel and ran into the owner, Greg Shockley. Greg greeted them and told them the Shoreham's ghost stories himself, which they enjoyed. I had a psychic on that tour, and she wanted to walk up to the second floor, so Greg showed them the way. The psychic said that the energy in the stairway and in the hall seemed to vibrate. She felt tingly and a sense of heaviness around her.

But we also had a nonbeliever on that tour. I'd invited him to attend, as he was the executive director of the Ocean City Development Corporation and an opinion leader in the town. I wanted him to experience the ghost walk personally so he could pass the word about our tours with enthusiasm. He stated at the very beginning that he didn't believe in ghosts. But he admitted that after walking up the stairs to the second floor, he could feel heaviness, a sort of constricting aura about the stairs and hall. He'd never felt anything like it.

After the guests returned from the second floor, Greg asked if they'd like to see the basement. The guests were thrilled. I stayed back, as there were plenty of soaking wet people already going in. When they came out, one of my guests was particularly distressed, but I didn't realize it until we left the Shoreham and huddled in a parking garage next door, where I finished the tour. I found out that while they were in the basement of the Shoreham, the lights went out. It freaked them all out because Greg explained how he had this switch that operated on a sensor installed so his employees wouldn't be so scared to go down there. As soon as someone entered the room, the sensor picked up the motion, and the lights came on. The lights would also go off by themselves when movement stopped for a period of time. But they mysteriously went off while the guests were in the room, and it evidently scared this guest so badly that she was having chest pains. She left with the friend who brought her and fortunately was feeling better the next day.

The presence in the Shoreham Hotel basement has some bad energy. I'm figuring it's best not to investigate or disturb it. The rest of the hotel has great energy with a bit of sadness in the hall on the second floor. Overall, it's a homey, friendly place with uplifting energy—especially in the very popular bar, Shenanigans, which fronts the Boardwalk. How could there be anything but powerful positive energy in an Irish bar? Who doesn't love Shenanigans?

PART II
BERLIN

The Town of Berlin (Worcester County) Arts and Entertainment District.

THE ATLANTIC HOTEL

The big, three-story Victorian hotel that spans a city block in Berlin's downtown is certainly the image that most brands the town. Everyone recognizes the Atlantic Hotel. It not only welcomes guests, but it also welcomes passersby with its collection of wide porch rockers on the veranda that borders the small plaza. The Atlantic Hotel is a meeting place, a stopping place and a place of gathering. There is probably no building in Worcester County that commands attention from visitors like this glorious building.

Horace Harmonson built the hotel in 1895 soon after a great fire consumed much of Berlin. Guests first arrived by stagecoach, and later the railroad brought visitors to town. Since Berlin was a place where the rail lines crossed, the town was a great stopping-off point for drummers—salesmen who pursued merchants and business owners to buy their wares (today's version would be wholesalers). Harmonson was also the Worcester County game warden, and he remained at the hotel with his family until his death in 1933. It wasn't uncommon for the hotel to have seasonal renters or long-term guests. The hotel has eighteen rooms and a cottage—and a fair number of spirits.

Probably the most familiar ghost story about the Atlantic Hotel is the one about a child haunting the second floor. A night clerk named Barbara was alone in the hotel. There were no guests on the second floor. She heard a loud dragging noise on the floor above her. It sounded as if some piece of furniture were being dragged from one end of the hall to the other. Though she was alone, she decided to investigate. She checked the hall, the side halls and the porches. There was no one on that floor, and nothing seemed out

The Atlantic Hotel in Berlin, built in 1895 by Horace Harmonson.

of order. When Barbara returned to her station, she heard the noise again, and again she investigated and found no one there. Later, Barbara shared her story with a Berlin native who knew a lot about the history and the hotel. She told Barbara that others had heard that noise, and it was believed to be the sound of a little girl riding her bike. The child lived in the hotel with her mother for a long time. People say she died in there and has haunted the hotel for years. Some people have seen her. Sometimes she bounces a ball. Occasionally, guests report hearing children laughing in the hallways late at night when the hotel is quiet.

The spirit of the little girl is also associated with Room 16. When the current owners of the hotel purchased it in 2009, all the rooms were gutted and redecorated. When the staff was redecorating the rooms, Room 16 smelled funny. The curtains were removed, as were the bedding and carpet. All the walls were scrubbed down, and try as they might, the staff couldn't eliminate the slight smell that was still in the room. When the staff was lining the dresser drawers with scented paper, the general manager was in Room 16, which stands across from Room 17. She noticed a little framed silhouette of George Washington in the drawer. It had no clasp on the back, and she wasn't yet prepared to be driving nails into the walls, as hanging pictures would be the last decorating task. So she propped George up on a little shelf that was on the dresser.

A week later, she and other staff members were adding necessary items to the dresser drawers such as blow-dryers and menus. The general manager was in Room 17. She opened the dresser to add the items and found a small gold-framed picture of a little blue-eyed girl. She had strawberry-blond hair and was wearing a blue dress. The general manager wondered how it got there because it hadn't been there the previous week when she'd lined the drawers. She thought the little girl might look good in Room 16, where she had previously found George Washington's silhouette. She carried the picture with the little girl across the hall to Room 16, hoping to switch it out with the silhouette of Washington that she'd placed on the dresser. But the silhouette was gone. She searched the dresser and the floor around it and then noticed that it was hung on the wall, despite it having had no clasp for hanging and despite there being no one authorized to hang pictures. It was unlikely that someone on the hotel staff would have hung the silhouette. They were so short staffed and in a rush to get the hotel open as it was. Hanging pictures wasn't a priority for anyone.

This picture of a little girl appeared in the dresser in Room 17 of the Atlantic Hotel. *Courtesy of the Atlantic Hotel.*

The general manager propped up the picture of the little girl on the dresser in Room 16, where it remains today. The room stopped smelling after the picture was placed there.

When the hotel first opened under its new ownership in 2009, a guest coming out of Room 16 approached the hotel manager and said, "Excuse me, do you work here?"

The manager replied, "Yes. What can I do to help you?"

The lady said, "There are no towels in my room."

The manager noted that this was a middle-aged woman who was small in stature. She had not seen this guest before, and she usually knew all of the guests. She asked the woman how many towels she needed, and the lady responded, "I have NO towels."

The manager was very surprised as this was an unlikely oversight. However, she gathered some fresh towels and brought them to Room 16. The door was ajar, so she rapped on the doorframe. There was no answer. She called out to the lady, not wanting to enter the room and startle her, but the lady still did not answer. So the general manager opened the door enough to put her face in the opening and called out again. There was still no answer. Finally, the general manager opened the door, thinking the lady might be in the bathroom, and still standing in the hall, she called out, "Ma'am, I have your towels. Do you want me to put them on your bed?" There was no answer.

The general manager decided to knock hard on the door, and suddenly the door flew open. She could see that there was no one in the room. She stepped into the room and checked the bathroom. The room was empty, and the bathroom was fully stocked with towels. She put the towels down on the bed and left quickly. She went down to the front desk to inquire about who was in Room 16. There was no one registered.

Room 16 in the Atlantic Hotel in Berlin.

There was another incident in Room 16 when a hotel staff person went up to check on a faulty air conditioner. Room 16 tends to have air-conditioning issues but not necessarily with the mechanics of the unit. It will switch itself off. There's never a problem with the heat, but the air conditioners are separate units. Often in the summer, the hotel staff will go up to Room 16 to turn the air conditioner on so the room will be cool when the guests arrive, and the unit will shut itself off. That room also has an issue with the door. The hotel management likes to leave the doors to the unoccupied guest rooms open so guests walking through the hotel can see what some of the rooms look like. Open doors provide light in the halls and offer a more welcoming atmosphere. The door in Room 16 never stays open. Though the staff will open all the doors and, in the case of Room 16, prop the door open with something, the door will end up closed and locked.

The registered guest in Room 16 said the air conditioner wasn't working. While the guest was out, the staff person went to Room 16 and entered the room, and the door slammed behind her with great force. These are not weighted doors like you find in newer hotels. The staff member said it seemed as if someone had slammed the door with great force. The room shook. Then she couldn't get the door open. She was trapped inside, and she panicked, screaming and banging on the door for someone to get her out of there. Within seconds, she realized she was in no danger; there was a phone in the room and plenty of people around. She phoned the front desk to ask for help, and when someone arrived, the door opened with no trouble. It didn't even stick.

The incidents in Room 16 are always prankish, like something a child would do. There's always been a story that a child died in Room 16 and still haunts the room, but there's no way to prove that. Horace Harmonson did have a daughter, but she grew into adulthood and is listed in the census records. But there were tenants who stayed in the hotel for months at a time during the Great Depression, and there are children listed in the census records as residing in the Atlantic Hotel. It's quite possible that a child could have once occupied the room, and there's plenty of spiritual activity to indicate there is a child spirit associated with this room today.

Barbara told a story of how the hotel managers decided to have a Christmas party for the employees. They chose a night during Christmas week when there were no guests in the hotel. They tried to make it as nice as possible. They had a dinner and were going to open gifts around the tree. Each employee had secretly chosen the name of another employee, and the tradition was to get one nice gift for that special person. There was one gift brought that evening that was wrapped especially well. It stood out from the others. The employee who opened that gift was thrilled. After the gifts were opened, everyone had drinks and chatted. As the party broke up and people went to get their coats and leave, the one gift that had been so beautifully wrapped was missing. They couldn't find it anywhere. Everyone pitched in to look all around—in the kitchen and dining room—but the gift had vanished. They decided to look the next day, and people began leaving.

Barbara was making preparations to close up when this middle-aged woman, who was very small in stature, came walking down the hotel staircase. This startled Barbara because there was no one registered in the hotel. The woman was holding the missing gift, which was beautifully wrapped the way it had been originally presented. She handed the gift to Barbara and walked out the door. She wasn't even wearing a coat.

Angela was standing in the hall with a clipboard in front of a table. There was a mirror above the table. She was making notes on the clipboard and felt something move behind her. She looked up in the mirror and noticed a shadow passing behind her. She turned around to see who was in the hall. There was no one in the hall, not from one end to the next. She went back to what she was doing and felt a presence behind her. Something was in the mirror. It looked like a shadow. It didn't frighten her, but she knew she wasn't alone.

Nina, who works the front desk, says that the lights over the desk will go out at will. Then they'll come on again later. This apparently happens only to Nina. Others at the front desk don't experience the lights going out. Another electronic abnormality that occurs when Nina is on duty is that the adding machine, which is stored under the counter, will start adding things. All of a sudden, the *tick-tick-ticking* of the numbers being totaled will sound off with no prompting. Nina was especially startled when the sound of the adding machine totaling up figures was heard when the machine was unplugged.

Room 18 is a big king room that can accommodate several people. A family was booked into Room 18 and called down to the front desk asking if they could change rooms. Nina asked if there was something wrong, and the guest said that she'd be right down. She explained that they were taking pictures of the family in the room, and they noticed that there was something other than their family in the picture. The guest also said they'd seen something that looked like beams of light dancing across the room. The hotel staff tried to smooth things over by saying it was probably just the reflection of the sun, but they rethought that when they realized this took place in the afternoon and that room doesn't get the afternoon sun. The family showed the picture to Nina and the staff and opted to move into another room.

The Atlantic Hotel is one of the three places where I had my own personal experience. It was quick, but it still makes me uneasy when I think about it. I was booked into Room 23 for one night with my husband. He had not yet arrived. The door was open as I approached the room—as all the unoccupied guest rooms were. When I crossed the threshold with bags in both hands, the door slammed shut behind me. It slammed with such force! I set the bags down to open the door back up and saw that the security bar, which one has to manually flip over the doorjamb, was already flipped over. I can't imagine how that could happen. My husband arrived; we had a wonderful dinner, and we loved our room. It was very comfortable. But for some reason, we couldn't sleep. Every time we'd begin to fall asleep, something would wake us up—startle us. Neither one of us got more than one consecutive hour of sleep that night.

When I was finishing up the writing of this book, I had to return to the Atlantic Hotel to retake the picture of Room 16. Every time I shot a picture of it, the image seemed to be blurry. I was ready. I had two lenses and a tripod. The housekeeping staff had just finished up in the room and were across the hall in Room 17. I explained what I was doing, and they politely motioned me into Room 16, but one of them said, "You know, you're never going to be able to keep that door open." I'd forgotten there was a problem with the door. While they were watching, I stepped inside, set down my things and pulled the door fully open so that it was touching the wall. It didn't move. Everyone watched. It stayed in place. I started setting up for the shoot, and about one minute into it, I heard the housekeeping staff all shout, "Look! Look, it's closing." The door was slowly shutting itself. I pulled it open again, and again it stayed open. I shot several pictures, and the housekeeping staff said goodbye and went down the hall with their cart and vacuum. About a minute later, the door slammed shut with such force that it shook the room.

I'm a believer.

The haunting of the Atlantic Hotel in Berlin is similar to the haunting of the Atlantic Hotel in Ocean City. The spirits are thick because the hotel has such a rich history. They are part of the Atlantic Hotel story, as are the guests who stay there today. It's likely that the spirits that stick around were once happy at the hotel or have some sense of belonging there. If they were mischievous in life, it's likely they are mischievous in the afterlife. The hotel has wonderful energy. It's an energy that connects with the past, where guests can feel as though they are stepping back in time as soon as they cross the threshold of that double-door entry. And though they might have to share the space with spirits of the past, there's room enough for everyone. We're all part of the Atlantic Hotel story.

THE INTERNATIONAL ORDER OF ODD FELLOWS

The Paran Hall, built by the International Order of Odd Fellows (IOOF) in 1902, is a mystical place. All Odd Fellows lodges have a mystical quality due to the rituals practiced in their meeting rooms—some with real human skeletons. These practices have been revealed publicly only in the last few decades as the IOOF fraternities have dissolved and their lodges have been taken over by private owners.

IOOF lodges existed in small towns all over America, and they follow a building style similar to the Paran Lodge. The halls, or lodges, were typically placed in the middle of town and had public space on the first floor and lodge meeting rooms on the upper floor. Sometimes, the first-floor public space was retail, and it could be leased out, bringing money to the lodge. In other cases, the public space might have been a community center used for meetings, dances and other public events. Access to the meeting hall was often through a separate street entrance with the Odd Fellows insignia carved over the doorway. The Paran Lodge in Berlin follows this model.

The retail storefront of the Paran Lodge faces South Main Street, while the meeting hall entrance faces Jefferson Street. Carved atop that doorway are the letters IOOF and a three-link chain, which is the symbol of the Odd Fellows fraternity. The three links stand for Friendship, Love and Truth—the things that bind the members to one another and illustrate that communities are strongest when they are joined together.

The Paran Lodge was built by the International Order of Odd Fellows in 1902.

Like the Masons and the Redmen, the Odd Fellows were a secret fraternal organization that assisted the less fortunate in the community. In Berlin, many of the prominent male citizens were members, including Calvin B. Taylor, Orlando Harrison and Dr. John Pitts. Other famous members of the IOOF were Winston Churchill, Wyatt Earp, Charlie Chaplin, Ulysses Grant, Franklin D. Roosevelt, Red Skelton and Burl Ives. The Odd Fellows were also one of the first fraternal organizations to admit women. Eleanor Roosevelt was a member, as was Georgia Dwelle, the first female African American physician.

The organization was founded in England in the 1600s; at that time, people in society were class conscious, and few helped their neighbors. When people got sick or loved ones died, families of the sick or deceased were left to fend for themselves. Many didn't have enough money for a doctor or to bury their own dead. The Odd Fellows began when a group of men stepped up and pooled their money together to help people in need. Since this attitude was contradictory to the way society thought at the time, they considered themselves "odd"—thus the name. They adopted a mission to welcome the stranger, educate the orphan, visit the sick, relieve the distressed and bury the dead.

There are small private cemeteries all over the Shore that are owned by the Odd Fellows. It's likely that the IOOF created these burial grounds to serve those who had no money to bury their dead.

Secrecy was imperative because if the public knew about the aid or assistance they were offering, someone would invariably try to sabotage the cause or usurp the pooled money. So passwords and secret handshakes and rituals were created so that members could identify who had been initiated into the order. Membership was divided into degrees based on the degree to which a member had demonstrated the fraternity's mission of leaving his own life behind and serving others in need. There was even a private club named the Ancient Mystic Order of Samaritans. The Odd Fellows had their rituals that specifically defined their mission.

Ritual practices alter the energy field in a place. When a human being meditates or concentrates while committing to ritual actions such as chanting, drumming or reciting a series of prayers or incantations, the energy field becomes charged with vibrations of intent. This often makes communication with the eternal world easier. Joint ritual practices—those where several people are chanting and meditating, magnifying this effect—can recharge old, dormant energies, connecting with the past. When certain symbolic charms or sacred objects—like stones, crucifixes or candles—are used during rituals, the shifting of energies can charge or electrify the objects, connecting them with energy from the other world. Simple demonstrations of this belief happen all the time in religions and fraternal organizations. Catholics believe that when a priest blesses a rosary, the rosary has a mystical or sacred quality about it that is to be respected and revered. Indigenous people of the Americas used elements of nature—stones, feathers, shells and pieces of bone—in their rituals, and they wore these items believing that they brought some type of blessing or protection.

The Odd Fellows used human skeletons in their rituals.

My friend Bob, who is an appraiser in Easton, said that when he was brought in to appraise the Easton IOOF lodge, he and the others with him were shown a drawer in a dais on the floor. When they opened the drawer, there was a human skeleton in it, laid out perfectly. Bob wondered what kind of weird rituals went on in that meeting hall. After hearing this, I did a little research and found that other lodges had skeletons or clusters of human bones.

Workers renovating the old IOOF lodge in Philadelphia began to rip out the old plaster walls to replace them with dry wall. As they pulled out the lath that supported the plaster, human skeletons fell out of the walls. The skeletons had been sealed into the walls when the building was constructed. While the IOOF kept its secrets and didn't reveal the purpose of the skeletons, experts suggested at the time that the skeletons had something to do with the vow each member took when he or she was accepted into the order, a vow that included a commitment to bury the dead. They weren't too far from the truth.

Every Odd Fellows lodge had a skeleton. Some of the skeletons may have been in actual coffins or in long drawers like the one in Easton. Some were tucked away in secret passages, and there are some lodges that simply had human bones tucked into a smaller casket. Over the years, as lodges closed, the skeletons were forgotten. Many have since turned up to the surprise of new property owners and their contractors. But it's important to remember that up until the 1950s, people could buy human skeletons, and there weren't such macabre associations attached to human remains. And the very belief demonstrated by the Odd Fellows in their rituals links the skeleton to human mortality and the passing away of the present world, looking to the higher existence—the eternal world.

Almost every IOOF lodge has the residual energy left in it from when the membership practiced a secret rite of passage using a real human skeleton. When a new member was about to be accepted into the first-degree level, that member was blindfolded and draped in chains. The blindfolded candidate was then led in a mock funeral procession with the rest of the membership trailing behind. The procession would end in the meeting hall, and all would gather around the blindfolded, chained candidate. A lodge member would remove the blindfold, and the candidate would be face to face with a human skeleton that was illuminated by two torches on either side. The candidate would be invited to meditate on his own mortality. The skeleton was a relic used in that sacred ritual—a relic that helped him focus on how quickly life fades, how we're here for only a short time, how death is imminent and there is a higher purpose for all of us and how his old way of life was dying, and from that day forward, he would embrace the mission of the International Order of Odd Fellows. The chaplain would offer prayers, and the candidate would place his right hand on his left breast and vow to keep the lodge's secrets, to abide by its rules and to never wrong a fellow lodge member or see him about to be wronged without warning him of the impending danger.

The Paran Lodge has a quiet, peaceful energy, especially on the upper floor where the meeting hall was. There was an art gallery in that space for a time that housed works from some of Worcester County's finest artists.

The yarn shop on the first level has brought a unique element of cheer to the town and become a place of congregation for local craftspeople. But occasionally, people sitting in the rocking chairs on the Atlantic Hotel's wide veranda next door have reported seeing a shadowy face looking out one of the upper-floor windows. The room is dark, and the face is not illuminated. The same shadow has appeared in photographs taken by guests on the ghost walk tours.

Considering the Paran Lodge was a place of fraternity where men came together, committed to support one another and practiced rituals marking rites of passage that elevated mortal awareness—rituals that incorporated human skeletons—it's not surprising that some energy left behind draws the old spirits back to a place where what they did mattered. These spirits in the Paran Hall are those that loved the town of Berlin; in life, they were committed to helping the less fortunate and to building a better, richer community.

AYERS GENERAL STORE

The Ayers General Store was built after the 1901 fire in Berlin. If you've
ever wondered why most historic American towns look alike with their
brick-front, flat-topped buildings, it's because around 1890, builders were
learning simple brick construction that was affordable. It made much more
sense to construct town buildings with brick because it was much more
resistant to fire. Buildings of wood perished, and all was lost if the fire
couldn't be brought under control quickly. Since the towns used brick one
hundred years ago, many buildings still stand, and the style of architecture is
that of the turn of the twentieth century. The Ayers General Store building
fits that style.

It was built to house two businesses, as one entrance faces South Main
Street and the other faces Bay Street. Mr. Ayers kept all kinds of things in
stock in his general store—tools, clothes, feed, paper. He was also known to
be fastidious about keeping the store clean and orderly. Today, the storefront
that faces Bay Street is the home of Baked Desserts Café, where delicious,
organic desserts are baked and served. One of the owners there said that
when she and her partner were renovating the store, they had some unusual
occurrences. Individually, the events could be explained away, but the fact
that they all occurred, and occurred repeatedly, gave them the sense that the
happenings were being generated in the spirit world.

Strange things began to happen during the renovations. One of the
most startling things was that the front doors, which are double doors
similar to French doors, would burst open. There was no wind behind

Ayers General Store, Bay Street entrance. Now home to Baked Desserts Café, it has a mischievous ghost.

them and no indication of why they should open with such force without assistance from a human. According to the owner, this happened often and still happens occasionally. There were also instances of bottles falling off the shelves, almost like dominos—again, with no apparent source for the movement. Electronic devices acted up. The radio would fade in and out, even on strong-frequency FM stations. There was an occasion when the electric fan started to spin faster than its normal set speed. The owners would shut everything off at night, close the bakery case, lock the doors and leave. In the morning, when they'd walk in, everything would be on— the lights, the fan, the radio—and the cases would be open. One time when this happened, the radio station had been changed to an AM station. The owner said she would have never switched the radio over to AM. They began to wonder if someone had the key and was coming in at night and rearranging things. There was never anything missing or destroyed. It seemed that electrical devices were going crazy.

One of the most startling times was when the owner's daughter was manning the store. She closed it up for the night but turned around when she was halfway home because she'd left something behind. She returned to the store within an hour of leaving it, and everything was on. All of the lights were turned on, as was the radio. The bakery case was open. The ceiling fan was rotating wildly. But the oddest thing of all was that the case for bottled drinks, which had a weighted door with an automatic close feature, was standing ajar by about four inches. The daughter shut it but could not duplicate the action.

The owner said that the activity slowed down once the renovations were complete. But there are still the occasional signs from whoever, or whatever, is haunting the place.

ADKINS HARDWARE
AND THE ELEMENTAL

The Adkins Hardware store in Berlin has been supplying everything needed for building since 1908. Its footprint by the railroad tracks on Harrison Street includes several storage buildings and a commercial store with offices. The store began as a sawmill and eventually expanded into selling lumber supplies and then all things necessary for builders. It had a convenient location, with its building set right on the railroad tracks. But a spark from the train ignited something near the building, and it caught fire and burned, so a new commercial building was erected away from the tracks in the 1970s. This is the main building for the store today. Adkins Hardware has been family owned since the beginning, and the fourth generation now manages the business.

Adkins Hardware has a ghost or two. The employees say that when the store is empty, they will hear in the aisles what sounds like a person moving things around on the shelves. They'll assume it's a customer they might have missed walking in. When they investigate, there is no one there. Several of them have had this experience. Sometimes they'll even hear a crash, like something falling off the shelves, and upon investigation, they discover no person and no trace of anything amiss.

The employees suspect that it is the spirit of Mr. Hudson, who used to run the store. He was very dedicated and kept everything at Adkins Hardware under tight control. One day, Hudson walked home for lunch and never

The Adkins Hardware store on Harrison Street is associated with three different ghost stories.

came back. He apparently died of a heart attack in his home that day. So the folks at Adkins Hardware figure maybe Mr. Hudson is still watching out for things. But there was another death—this one on Adkins property—that happened in the 1930s. According to a life-long Berlin resident, a man who was caught stealing money hanged himself down where the mill was located at the time. Maybe the unrestful spirit of this unfortunate man is still looking for peace—and prowling the aisles of the store.

Another strange occurrence happened in the offices, this one totally unrelated to the phantom walker in the aisles. The man who currently runs Adkins Hardware talked of a special clock that was given to his grandfather Roland Powell. When Powell ran the hardware business years ago, he received a beautiful clock as a gift from his friend Elton Richardson, who had handcrafted the clock. Richardson's clocks were rare, and he made them only for special friends. The clock sat in a prominent place in Mr. Powell's office, and it still sits in the Adkins Hardware office. On the day Elton Richardson died, the clock stopped at the exact time he died, and the door on the front of the clock popped open, which it had never done before.

Perhaps the entire Adkins complex has a mystical quality. In a grassy area between two storage buildings, there have been sightings of an elemental, or nonhuman, spirit. The term *elemental* means "of the elements" or "of the basic core of natural existence, evolved from the four realms of earth, wind, fire and water." All nonhuman spirits we've read and heard about such as angels, fairies, banshees, shadow people, elves, gnomes, brownies and pixies are elementals.

A man I interviewed about another property called me after our interview and said he wanted to tell me about what he and his girlfriend experienced down near Adkins Hardware. His girlfriend lives in Berlin, and he was driving her home. They stopped on Harrison Street near Adkins Hardware to finish a conversation. It was dusk, and the daylight was almost gone. The man noticed a shadow on the grass—a black shadow, but not like a person's shadow. It was more like a black, shapeless form. It moved across the grass, and then it vanished. They were intrigued and decided to come back another time to see if they could glimpse it again and perhaps take a few pictures. On a subsequent visit, they did see the elemental again. They tried to photograph it, but the cameras were dead. Then they noticed it coming toward the car, and they were frightened and left. The man said he'll never go back. He won't even drive down Harrison Street.

Adkins Hardware is a stop on the Berlin Ghost Walk, and it is one of the most common places where guests will get strange anomalies in their photo images. Orbs, flashes, laser-like lights and shadows are common. It's a mystical place.

THE HEALING TREE

Everything is made of energy. And energy is the life force that runs through every living thing. There is a certain sycamore tree in Berlin that some believe emits an energy that is healing; if you stand in the energy field of the tree, you can absorb some of the tree's life force, and that force can actually change or alter cells in the body and create a healing effect.

This two-hundred-year-old sycamore is a tree of a thousand faces. If you approach it at night and shine a light on it, the faces will appear. There is a large smiling face on the trunk, another on an exposed root by the sidewalk and many, many faces among its branches. It sits on Main Street in front of the Calvin B. Taylor House Museum, and its massive trunk is curved, giving it the look of constant motion. In the winter, when this tree has lost its leaves, it appears to be dancing.

People who work in the healing arts, such as herbalists, Reiki masters and massage therapists, will come to this tree and stand in its presence, lean on it or sit beneath it. They believe that they can absorb the healing energy from this tree and give back their own energy in a sort of spiritual dialogue that strengthens both parties. Trees and humans have a unique reciprocal relationship anyway. The tree breathes in the carbon dioxide that we exhale, and we breathe in the oxygen that it releases. The healing energy exchange is similar, and this is a powerful tree.

Trees themselves have a mystical quality that has been revered by many cultures. British explorers who studied certain tribal communities noted that when a tribe wanted to fell a tree, the men or warriors of the tribe would

This two-hundred-year-old sycamore tree in the yard of the Calvin B. Taylor House Museum is believed to have mystical properties.

choose a tree and violently scream at it for hours. They'd repeat the practice of yelling angrily at the tree for weeks, and the tree would die. Then they would simply push it over. The tree absorbs the bad energy, the negative karma, the breach in the sacred, spiritual dialogue between humans and itself. So it dies. The same concept rings true in studies that show that when people talk to plants, they grow stronger.

If you hold your hand up to this tree and leave about an inch or two between the tree and your palm, you will be able to feel the vibration of the energy the tree is releasing. It may feel like heat, it may feel like a tingling, but if you still your mind and focus on the tree, you will feel that healing power that the tree gives off. Some attribute this tree's healing energy to it being located on a ley line, or a pulsating vein of energy running through the earth. A ley line is like a radio frequency. We can't see it, but we know it's there, and it provides a connection between transmitting sources. We can identify ley lines similarly to how dowsers or diviners find water with a dowsing rod or forked branch. These methods for identifying water sources have been practiced in cultures all over the world for centuries.

Trees that grow on ley lines tend to draw the energy from that ley line and absorb it, giving them extra strength to thrive, grow and fight off

The Calvin B. Taylor House, now a museum focused on the history of Berlin.

disease. They also tend to split and grow on either side of the ley line they are straddling.

There is a sacredness attributed to sycamore trees. The Indians called them ghost trees because of the way their light-colored bark stood out in the landscape during the winter months. Their speckled bark absorbs the moonlight, which reflects off the trees. Sycamores are revered in Egypt. Egyptians believed a wand or staff fashioned from a sycamore could draw the energies of Hathor, the Egyptian "mother" goddess, into one's own energy field and promote healing and connection to nature and advance the gifts of the mind and spirit. The *Egyptian Book of the Dead* states that twin sycamores stand on either side of the Gate of Heaven.

In the movie *The Karate Kid*, Mr. Miyagi teaches young Daniel about "chi," or the life force that moves within us. Harnessing the chi gives us power from within. The mingling of our energy with the healing tree's energy is kind of a dual chi. The life force running through us mingles with the life force running through the tree. And we strengthen each other.

So if you have the opportunity to stand in the presence of this mystical sycamore tree in Berlin, place your hand on the trunk and draw in the life force. If you have an illness or a need for healing, leave it with the tree. You may be surprised at how much better you feel afterward.

BERLIN'S WALKING DEAD

B erlin is one of the few towns on the Eastern Shore where residents have claimed to see spirits or ghosts walking the streets. In other towns, like Snow Hill, St. Michaels or Pocomoke, there have been sightings of spirits walking the streets, but in those cases, it was only one spirit or one witness. In the Folklore Collection at the Edward H. Nabb Research Center, there were two mentions of spirit sightings on the Berlin streets. Another sighting was relayed through interviews with residents who live in the second-floor apartments in the commercial downtown buildings. All three cases were by different informants and given over a period of thirty years. Still, this is an unusual coincidence for one small town. What is it that makes the dead want to walk the streets of Berlin?

While it's true that Berlin has one of the most beautiful downtowns on the Peninsula—so beautiful that it has been chosen as the set for two Hollywood movies—attractive streetscapes haven't been a common draw for spirits to manifest themselves in the form of full-blown apparitions. What's equally interesting about these three apparitions is that all three seem to have a different purpose. One is waiting for someone. One is parading, wanting to be noticed. And one is apparently lost, either physically or lost in thought. So there is no common event like soldiers on a battlefield and no common purpose like children playing in a schoolyard.

The first sighting is simple: one person, one place. A woman wearing white was seen by the residents in the second-floor apartments near Main and Pitts Streets. She stood next to the Calvin B. Taylor Bank. One resident says that he saw her there late at night from his window. The streets in Berlin's retail commercial district are empty by nine o'clock at night. So it was odd to see a lady standing there next to the bank. The man said that his roommate saw her, too, but only briefly before she vanished. Later, the second-floor resident saw her again when he came out of the building one night to take a walk. He said he saw her as clear and as real as any human being. But she was wearing a long white dress and had her brown hair pulled up the way women wore their hair in the 1920s. She appeared to be waiting for something or someone. She was looking from side to side up and down Main Street. For an instant, he thought she was a real person and that maybe she needed help like a ride or something. He started to cross the street to talk with her, and he said she looked straight at him and then vanished. After that, they never saw her again.

The account of the second sighting came from the Folklore Collection. It is of a Confederate soldier who was seen walking down Main Street in Berlin at night. He was dressed in his gray uniform with a slouch hat. He walked as if he were in a parade, standing tall with his head held high, looking from

The Calvin B. Taylor Bank in Berlin, where the Lady in White has been seen waiting for something or someone.

115

side to side as if he were acknowledging spectators. While the informant saw the soldier on Main Street, his father saw the soldier walking down Baker Street and others saw the soldier on Williams Street.

The Pitts family of Berlin did have two family members serve in the Confederate army. Both were in the Virginia Cavalry serving under J.E.B. Stuart. Fred Pitts was at the Battle of Yellow Tavern in 1864, just north of Richmond. It was there that he caught the mortally wounded Major General J.E.B. Stuart as he fell from his horse. Pitts carried Stuart off the battlefield and held him in the rear of the company, preventing Stuart's capture by Union forces. Fred Pitts also was present at the surrender at Appomattox Courthouse. John W. Pitts served in the Confederate Infantry and later with the Virginia Cavalry under Stuart, but upon returning from the war, he practiced medicine. He became the town doctor and was also Berlin's first mayor. He served as vice-president of the Calvin B. Taylor Bank and was the district deputy grand master of the Independent Order of Odd Fellows.

The third sighting was relayed in an interview with a seventy-year-old woman who had lived in Berlin all of her life. She said that she saw Ned France shuffling down the center of Main Street in the early morning hours before the commercial district was awake. She said that in the summer, she would take her walk just after the sun came up and while the downtown streets were empty. One morning, she saw this man in a light-colored suit that was slightly baggy. He was walking up Main Street with his head bowed down, and he walked with a shuffle. She recognized that shuffle and believed the man was Ned France. But Ned had been dead for years. She knew Ned when he was alive and said she'd recognize that walk anywhere. He was walking in front of where his famed Uncle Ned's Bargain Fair used to stand.

Ned France had a secondhand store on Main Street where he sold all kinds of junk. He had furniture, household supplies and old tools. He also had strange things like a human skeleton, a suit of armor and false teeth. Ned's was the place where music lovers could buy 45rpm records, but several people in the town who remember having to go into Ned's to buy records as teenagers admit that Ned was a little strange. Sometimes he scared them. Ned also contracted himself out as a magician and provided entertainment at kids' birthday parties. He once did a Houdini-type escape act in public when he hung himself, bound in chains, in an upside-down position from a store awning across from the Atlantic Hotel. He managed the escape perfectly. One Berlin local said he needed a push broom and was walking to the hardware store on Main Street that was located just down from Ned's to buy one. He said that Ned crept up behind him and, while walking, started muttering, "Good push brooms at Ned's...Good push brooms at Ned's."

The Calvin B. Taylor Museum House has a good collection of Ned France memorabilia, including advertising posters and some of his magic act equipment. Another artifact it has in the Ned France collection is a piece of electronic equipment he used when holding séances. He would connect the apparatus to the lights in the room where everyone was gathered. He would place it under the séance table, and when he would gently (and inconspicuously) tap the apparatus with his foot, the lights would go out, leaving those gathered around the table believing that the lights going out was a sign from the spirits they were summoning.

As Ned got older, his wife passed away, and it became more difficult for him to manage the store. He sold the store and eventually moved into an assisted living facility. The Berlin town manager said that Ned used to call there from the assisted living facility and ask them to come and get him. He said he didn't belong there, that he wanted to come home and they wouldn't let him go.

Such is the story of many broken spirits that try to make their way back home. The building that once housed Ned's Bargain Fair has been torn down, and a new building stands in its place. During one of the Berlin ghost walks, there was a guest who had an electronic voice phenomena (EVP) recorder. Occasionally, the recorder would generate a word or a phrase, and a recorder voice would project that word or phrase. As we were standing in front of that replacement building where Ned's Bargain Fair once stood, I told the Ned France story. When I said that some people believe Ned France is still walking the streets of Berlin, the EVP recorder generated and played the word "True." Later in the story, when I told about the guy who wanted a push broom and Ned France was following him saying, "Good push brooms at Ned's," the EVP recorder said, "That was fun." Those were the only two times the recorder delivered any words or phrases on that tour.

Here's to Ned France and all the unrestful spirits who just want to go home.

DAIRY QUEEN BUILDING

Next to the building that replaced Uncle Ned's Bargain Fair and across the street from the public parking lot that hosts the Berlin Farmers Market is a small, one-story building that was constructed in an alleyway. It used to be a Dairy Queen, but in recent years it has been a bakery.

Roberta Ward, the owner of the Pink Box Bakery, which operated from this building a few years ago, said that the building was haunted while she was there. Strange things would happen with the electricity. An oven would just stop working while baking and then start up again later. Lights would go off in the bakery and then come back on. She said people would call her at home in the evenings and let her know that the bakery lights were on when she was positive she'd shut them off before leaving. On more than one occasion, she came into the bakery in the early morning, and the back door was wide open. Nothing was ever missing or vandalized—just a wide open door that she was sure she had secured before leaving.

One day, her assistant, Erica, was washing down the stainless-steel prep table with a soapy cloth. Then Erica went to rinse the cloth and wipe down the table again. When she returned to the prep table, there were strange hieroglyphics drawn into the soap. She'd left the counter only for seconds—the amount of time that it takes to rinse a cloth. Erica was frightened by the incident.

But the strangest occurrence of all was that both Roberta and Erica occasionally saw cats in their peripheral vision. Out of the corners of their eyes, they would notice a cat jump or move, but when they looked directly at

The old Dairy Queen, now a bakery on Berlin's Main Street.

where the cat should have been, it wasn't there. They could see them only in their peripheral vision. When they began asking questions about why they might be seeing cats, a local person told them that the fish market used to be across the street.

Roberta said she loved the building and that it had a wonderful, warm energy. She so enjoyed the time she spent there, but she added, "I never felt that I was alone in that building."

WINDY BROW

The old homeplace of Orlando Harrison, built in 1899, sits across from the railroad tracks in Berlin and very near where the old passenger station stood. The house has no haunted story that we know of, but if ever there was a house that radiated the spirit and charisma of a family, it would be Windy Brow. The Harrison story is a wonderful tale of the dead.

It's the story of Orlando Harrison and peaches and rail cars and the people who worked for the Harrison Brothers Nurseries (the brothers being Orlando and George). The Harrisons had an impact on the lives of hundreds of Worcester Countians and thousands of their descendants. Futures were shaped and millionaires made because of the business that Orlando Harrison built at this location. The Harrison contribution to Berlin generated enough wealth that many in the town were able to lead comfortable, happy lives. And we all know that spirits tend to return to where they were most happy and fulfilled. We can thank Orlando and the rest of the Harrison clan for indirectly accelerating the growth of what would become a very haunted town.

Orlando was born in Roxana, Delaware, in 1867 to a farmer who moved the family to Worcester County in 1884. Orlando worked alongside his father in the farming business, and at a young age, he began studying new techniques for grafting and growing fruit trees. He was apparently brilliant, and it was that intellect and savvy business sense that helped Orlando propel his family's nursery business into one of the most successful farming families in Worcester County history.

The Windy Brow Harrison homestead in Berlin, built by Orlando Harrison.

In 1893, as the business was growing, Orlando Harrison married Ada Long, who was from Frankford, Delaware. They had four sons: G. Hale Harrison, Henry L. Harrison, Orlando Jr. and John Long Harrison. Their eldest, G. Hale, graduated from Cornell University and was the first to assume some of his father's responsibilities, which freed up time for Orlando to participate in public service. Orlando served as a representative in the Maryland House of Delegates, completed several terms as mayor of Berlin and was elected a Maryland state senator.

Eventually, Harrison Brothers Nurseries became the largest grower and distributor of fruit trees, shade trees and ornamental shrubbery in the world. It was probably best known, however, for its peaches.

Author Joe Moore, who is also a native of Berlin and an avid historian, said that when he was little, the road from Berlin to Snow Hill (Route 113) was nothing but peach orchards. For miles and miles, as far as you could see, there were Harrison Brothers peach orchards—or at least it seemed that way. Windy Brow was built as the Harrison family success story began to peak. The barns and equipment for the business were behind the house, and the old railroad depot across from the house was commonly occupied by railcars loaded with hundreds of bushels of Harrison peaches and produce ready to be shipped out to markets in the big cities. Windy Brow was the beautiful and ornamental focal point of the Harrison spirit.

Harrison Brothers Nurseries dominated the U.S. peach market and generated between 250 and 500 jobs in and around Berlin, depending on the season. Even by today's standards, that's a very large employer for the Eastern Shore. For over forty years, Orlando Harrison paid out higher wages annually than any other man in Worcester County.

When George died, Orlando ran the business with men from the next generation of Harrisons, including his own four sons and George's two sons. Each had a special area of focus, and the seven of them grew the company in epic proportions to the point where they were producing ten million trees and seedlings in a year. After a lifetime of service to the nurseries, the public and his family, Senator Orlando Harrison died in 1928. He was sixty-one years old. The company continued under the leadership of his sons and nephews.

In the 1960s, a devastating peach blight wiped out the Harrison orchards. Most of the Harrison Brothers assets were lost, but Windy Brow stayed soundly within the family. At that time, the Harrison patriarch was Orlando's son G. Hale, who had already started to diversify by investing in the hospitality industry in Ocean City. G. Hale built the Harrison Hall hotel in the 1950s as a gift to his wife, Lois. Once the orchards were lost, G. Hale and Lois focused on building their hotel business. And they were remarkably successful, partly because Ocean City was growing and spreading northward due to the increase of travelers coming by automobile over the new Chesapeake Bay Bridge.

When G. Hale died, he left his wife, Lois, with three young children. Lois took over the hotel business and trained her children in the principles of success in the hospitality industry. When they were barely in their twenties, Lois's two sons—Hale and John—purchased the Plim Plaza Hotel, which today serves as the headquarters of the Harrison Group. This company operates ten oceanfront resort hotels and twelve restaurants. It's quite a legacy that the grandsons of Orlando Harrison have built.

Windy Brow still occupies the space where Orlando Harrison placed it in 115 years ago. And though Orlando and his wife, Ada, have passed on, as have G. Hale and Lois, a third generation has taken ownership and are creating a new Harrison legacy.

To the Harrisons, Windy Brow will always be the old homestead. But to Berliners, it's not only a reminder of the contributions made by Orlando Harrison and his descendants, who went from farming success to being hotel magnates, but also a testimony to a town that was built on peaches and successfully transitioned into a town that rests on the shoulders of the tourism industry.

The spirits of all those Harrisons culminate at Windy Brow, but the spirits of the Berliners who worked for the Harrisons and who benefitted from the Harrison success are all around the town.

RACKLIFFE HOUSE

J ust across the Inlet from Ocean City and a few miles inland on Assateague Island are the grounds of an old Indian settlement. Excavations have uncovered evidence that shows there were Indians on this land ten thousand years ago. This marks one of the oldest indigenous settlements in America—older, even, than the pyramids of Egypt. Eventually, colonial settlers drove the Indians off this land in order to settle it themselves. In the 1740s, Captain Charles Rackliffe built the brick structure known today as the Rackliffe House. It was part of a large plantation, and Charles Rackliffe had many slaves. The property continued to pass through Rackliffe descendants all the way into the 1930s, when the final descendant died at the house after nearly ten years of being bedridden. He had no legitimate children. Tenants took over the house until it fell into such disrepair that it was uninhabitable. Today, the house has been restored by a nonprofit committed to its preservation and is open to the public as a museum.

The house had views of the sea and was set on hundreds of rolling acres of field and forest. The Rackliffes were wealthy. They were prominent in the local society, and the house was a hub for social activities. There was a room dubbed the "ballroom," and it had oak floors designed so that the planks were loosely placed, which offered a kind of spring effect as feet moved about the floor. This made it easier on the dancers' feet. The Rackliffes built their house intending it to be a meeting place for high society—as high as society could get in the colonial coastal bay region. There surely would have been a lot of comings and goings of people in that house over the years.

Rackliffe House, built by Captain Charles Rackliffe about 1740.

But Rackliffe House has more stories of hauntings and unexplained events than any other property in Worcester County. Residents, neighbors, tenant farmers, golfers and visitors to the house have offered accounts over the years of strange happenings at Rackliffe House, and the stories keep coming. There have also been several paranormal investigations performed inside, and all gathered strong evidence linked to supernatural occurrences. There are three stories in the house's history that are violent. And like the Shoreham Hotel in Ocean City, the Rackliffe House hit the haunted trifecta by being the site of a murder, a suicide and an accidental death.

When Captain Charles Rackliffe died in 1752, his son John inherited the property. After John's death, the property was passed to his son—also John. This John was known to be particularly brutal to his slaves. His brutality caught up with him, though; legend has it that John Rackliffe, son of John and grandson of Captain Charles Rackliffe, was ambushed by his slaves as he was returning home one night. He was apparently stabbed to death. He left behind his wife, Sarah, and their four children. Shortly after that, a female guest attending a party at the Rackliffe House and wearing elegant clothing apparently tripped while descending the stairs. She took the fall hard and died from her injuries. Then, Sarah Rackliffe died not long after her husband, John. Some say the slaves murdered her, too, by poisoning the butter. When Sarah died, the four Rackliffe children were left orphans.

There's also a story about a Rackliffe House widow who lost her son to the British during the War of 1812. During this time, the British sailed up the Chesapeake and Coastal Bays. They would sometimes stop at farms and plantations along the waterway and snatch young local men in order to press them into military service. There was an older widow living at Rackliffe House with her son. The British landed at Rackliffe House, found the widow's son and decided to take him on board and force him to serve in their navy. The widow begged the British captain not to allow his men to take her son. She pleaded, saying that her son was all that she had in the world. But her pleas had no influence on the British captain. They took the boy on board. The widow, who was then left all alone, fell into despair. She hanged herself in the attic.

Much of the commentary we have about the mysterious, unexplained events at Rackliffe House comes from Denise Milko, owner of Holiday Real Estate in Ocean City. Denise lived at Rackliffe House as a teenager and young adult. She describes her years there as being where some of her happiest memories were made. There was a twenty-stall barn on the property when she lived there, and her family kept horses. She remembers how exhilarating it was to ride her horses all around that seaside landscape. She felt spiritually connected to both the house and the land, and perhaps her spiritual openness was why she experienced so many strange things. But Denise wasn't the only one who experienced unexplained events. Over the years, so many different people either experienced or observed supernatural occurrences there that the Rackliffe House got the reputation for being haunted.

Denise said that animals were particularly sensitive to a shift in energy. Sometimes the horses would stir. They would be agitated in their stalls for no apparent reason. They sensed something that she and her parents couldn't see. Those were usually the nights when something mysterious would happen. There were weather phenomena that would occur around the house. The wind would kick up, rain would come and then the wind would shift in a way that seemed as though the violent weather were swirling around Rackliffe House, going in all directions. There were times when Denise would hear dogs barking outside the house, but when she investigated, there were no dogs. There were also sounds of horses galloping down the lane, but there were never any horses that came into view. There were dogs that came with

A quarter-mile wooded path leading to the Rackliffe House from the Assateague Island Visitor Center.

visiting guests that seemed to sense something. One Labrador retriever in particular refused to climb the stairs. On one occasion, Denise's dog became so agitated that he gave Denise a serious bite when she was trying to calm him. The animals there were always sensitive to other realms and the eternal world, and their behavior sometimes suggested that spirits from the other realms were present.

When Denise's aunts were visiting and staying overnight at the house, their niece remembers sitting at breakfast and having them ask her what she was doing all night making such a racket. It sounded like she was moving furniture and banging on something. It kept waking them up. Denise's mother admitted to hearing it as well. Her mother added that every time she went to Denise's room to ask her to stop, the lights were off and Denise was sleeping. Denise said there were weird things that would happen in her room. Sometimes she'd go into her room and find all of the drawers open. Things would go missing. She had a favorite hand mirror that disappeared one day. She knew she'd left it on the dresser. When she did locate her hand mirror, it was cracked.

Sometimes, Denise and her family could hear the piano playing by itself. Also, they could sometimes hear soft footsteps around the house, especially in the ballroom. Members of the family would hear someone call their names and not be able to locate the caller. And there would occasionally be the smell of perfume on the stairway and in the ballroom. In a small room off one of the bedrooms, they could sometimes hear the faint sound of a baby crying. These kinds of things happened so often that, after a while, they became commonplace for Denise and her parents. At a family celebration, a large group of family members were gathered around the table in the dining room, and Denise's mother began to talk about these unexplained events. One of the family members said that he didn't believe in ghosts. In that instant, all of the electric lights in the house went out, and the lit candles on the table flared up. The room was silent, and the guests sat in shock. Then the lights came back on, and the candles flared again.

Denise also found that African American people she knew wouldn't go down the Rackliffe House lane at night. They wouldn't say why, but there was a feeling they had. They were fearful of something on the land at night. A golf pro who worked at the golf course near the house said that when he was passing by, he heard a loud crash coming from the house and described it as sounding like a piano being dropped from the second floor. When he investigated a little closer, there was nothing out of order. And the piano was fine.

Denise said that the only time she got really scared and felt unsafe was one night when she was home alone. Her parents were nearby, working at their store, and Denise was studying in her room. Her dogs were with her. She heard what sounded like close gunfire followed by the loudest crash of glass she'd ever heard. She assumed someone had shot out one of the house's windows. She called her father and the police from the phone in her room, and they both arrived quickly. They searched the house and the property. There was absolutely no evidence of any gunfire and no broken glass found in or near the house.

Paranormal investigators who investigated Rackliffe House on two separate occasions gathered a good amount of evidence indicating supernatural activity.

The last Rackliffe descendant to live at Rackliffe House was James Dirickson. He never married and lived as a bachelor with a housekeeper who was also likely his mistress. Her name was Martha Hargrow, and she was a biracial farm laborer. She also served as Dirickson's caregiver during his last ten years when he was bedridden. Dirickson died at Rackliffe House in 1902, but some feel that he is still present. During one paranormal investigation, an investigator named Missy commented to the other investigators that Mr. Dirickson must have had a lonely existence being bedridden for so long prior to his death. Missy got a reading on the EVP directly after she made that comment. It was a male voice saying, "I'm still here."

During the first investigation Missy did, she said she felt a spirit pass right through her—from her head to her toes:

> *I felt a tingling sensation that started at the top of my head and ended at the tip of my toes. It went completely through my body. It was peaceful but intense. It then went through* [the other investigator] *and then through his wife. The air was static. Once more after that, we could all feel the static within our bodies, but not as intensely as the first "pass through" event, if that is what it was. I know in my heart that it was. I have never felt anything like that before or since, and it is a difficult sensation to explain.*

Missy also said that something touched her during the Rackliffe House investigation. It felt like a brushing across her neck.

Other tenants at Rackliffe House had experiences that mirror the effects of a poltergeist. These tenants had framed artwork that they arranged on the wall. When they returned home one day, the artwork was removed from the wall and piled onto the floor. They rehung the pictures. Again, the pictures were mysteriously removed from the wall, but this time the artwork, which had been custom framed with a sealed backing, was reversed behind the glass and upside down with no evidence of the glass or sealed backing having been tampered with. The same couple also came home to find their newly hung drapes spread out on the floor, perpendicular to the windows.

So why does all of this happen at Rackliffe House? Why don't all of the other plantation houses in Worcester County have such crazy supernatural activity? Based on the history we actually do know and the history we suspect is true, we can assume that the property is associated with sadness and violence. We know that the Assateague Indians who lived in this region were a peaceful people and that the Indians who lived at Rackliffe House imprinted the landscape with the spirit of their tribe. They buried their dead on this land, and as the bones of their ancestors turned to dust, the earth beneath Rackliffe House became charged with the DNA of a people who called the land home for over ten thousand years. We know that Anglo settlers intruded, occupied the land, made empty promises and eventually drove the Indians out.

We know that the Rackliffes settled here, built the Rackliffe House and operated a thriving plantation, but they did so on the backs of slaves. There were slaves who lived and died here and are likely buried in unremembered, unmarked graves on the property. We suspect that John Rackliffe tortured his slaves and was eventually murdered by them. We also suspect that the slaves may have murdered Sarah Rackliffe. We know that the four Rackliffe children were left orphaned. We know that James Dirickson spent years in the house, sick and bedridden with very little company.

So the landscape and the house are marked with the anguish of an exiled people, the oppression of people who were enslaved and tortured, the terror of a man ambushed and murdered on his way home, the possible murder of a mother who left behind four young children and the sense of abandonment felt by children who lost both parents. That much we know based on documentation and strong local legend. Add to that the possible suicide of a widow and the accidental death of a young woman, and it becomes apparent that the energy field around this house has been burned with the imprint of human suffering. And that imprint opens doors to the otherworld, to realms beyond the physical realm we live in. That portal or open door allows spirits to move more freely, to use less energy to manifest themselves in our realm. It allows not only past spirits associated with the property to move between worlds but elemental, poltergeist and nonhuman spirits to move in as well.

Perhaps Rackliffe House is so active with spirits because it has an open doorway to that eternal world.

THE ASSATEAGUE INDIAN

Artist Peter Toth carved the twenty-foot-tall Indian sculpture at Inlet Park in 1976 from a one-hundred-year-old oak tree. It was part of his mission to raise awareness of the plight of America's indigenous people. This wooden Indian sculpture that greets visitors who enter the Inlet parking lot is part of Toth's "Trail of the Whispering Giants," which is composed of at least one carved Indian in every one of the United States. This sculpture is Peter Toth's gift to Maryland.

Most of Toth's sculptures still survive across the fifty states. Every one is unique, and each was carved on-site by Toth and given to the locality as a gift. Many are familiar with Toth's Delaware sculpture, *Chief Little Owl*, the twenty-seven-foot-tall Indian totem pole that greets visitors entering Bethany Beach.

Toth named the Maryland sculpture at the Inlet *The Assateague Indian*. The sculpture is placed so that the Indian faces Assateague Island—a place where the Assateague Indians lived for thousands of years. This sculpture is said to have mystical properties. At first glance, the Indian's face seems expressionless. But local people say that if you sit quietly and stare into the face of the sculpture, you will start to cry within ten minutes. It took me only three minutes.

There is so much pain in the face of the Assateague Indian. His wrinkled brow, his distant eyes and the slight frown all exhibit such sadness. The Indian himself appears to be crying.

Sadly, this sculpture is decaying; it will soon be beyond repair and fall apart. The elements of nature on the Atlantic coast have taken their toll. It

The Assateague Indian, carved by Peter Toth from a one-hundred-year-old oak as part of his "Trail of the Whispering Giants."

has been repaired once, but repairing it a second time is too costly, and there are no funds to support restoration. So here's to *The Assateague Indian*. Visit him while you can, and see if he can make you cry.

AFTERWORD

When I was little, like all youngsters in Maryland, I loved to go to Ocean City. My uncle had a trailer in Montego Bay near 130th Street, and every year he'd invite me to stay for a week or two with him. Those weeks spent with the Granados clan in Ocean City make up some of my best childhood memories. I made more memories as a parent when I brought my own children to the beach. Like most kids, mine could stay on the beach from sunrise to sunset, but the real excitement came from the anticipation about what we would do in the evening: go to the Boardwalk.

If you ask my kids what they remember about summers at the beach, they'll say playing with their cousins and going to the Boardwalk. T-shirts and hermit crabs for sale, funnel cakes, bumper cars, the shooting gallery and ice cream at Dumser's—these little flashes are great family memories. Perhaps memories of the Boardwalk are so vivid because they engage every one of our five senses. The smell of Fisher's popcorn and the vinegar on Thrasher's French fries, the rumble in the tummy from spinning on the Tilt-a-Whirl, the softness of the plush fur on the stuffed animal won at an arcade game, the music of the carousel, the screams from the haunted house and a panoramic view set in a landscape of ocean, sand and sky, dotted with the lights of the Ferris wheel and the movement of one thousand people who are having the time of their lives. This is the Ocean City Boardwalk experience for a child. Whether we remember it as children or as parents who watched that magic unfold before our own kids, times spent in Ocean City color our lives happy.

Postcard of the Atlantic Hotel in Ocean City.

When I started this book, I thought I knew Ocean City. How wrong I was. To find the ghost stories one must uncover the history. I never thought of Ocean City as a historic town. I didn't know any of the history. And so I spent a month searching for the stories, with two little eight-year-old granddaughters who were spending the summer with us. Together we searched. I took them on interviews. We visited dozens of sites. We met prominent Ocean City people and heard their stories. A whole new Boardwalk experience was born. How much more interesting the life-saving station becomes when you know that Laughing Sal sometimes laughs on her own and that there are the spirits of sailors and children lurking around. Mia and Gracie will never ride Trimper's Carousel again without saying hello to Miss Joanne and hoping they can catch the scent of her perfume. They never knew that there was a time when people of color weren't allowed to stay in the same hotels as everyone else—a sad part of our history to learn but one that unfolds when you hear the story of the Henry Hotel. They loved hugging the stone marker at Captain's Hill, hearing about shipwrecks, looking for the shadow in the mirror at the Atlantic Hotel and staring at *The Assateague Indian* to see how long it would take before they cried. We will never forget that summer we learned about the ghosts in Ocean City.

This year, the town of Berlin received the "Coolest Town in America" recognition from *Budget Travel* magazine. The competition was tough, and hundreds of thousands of people weighed in when it came time to vote. Who doesn't love Berlin? It's got everything you'd ever want in a small town—fabulous architecture, wonderful shopping, a farmers market, great food, a tearoom, three bakeries (at last count), tree-lined streets, free Wi-Fi and friendly people. Easy access from Ocean City has always made Berlin popular with tourists.

But like Ocean City, the Berlin experience is so much richer when you know the stories of the people who lived there when the town was built—and still live there. Berlin has such colorful spirits haunting the streets, the stores and the hotel. The Atlantic Hotel alone is so haunted that one can scarcely spend a day there without running into some kind of spirit. Berlin is a mystical town—a town to see slowly. Take in what surrounds you with thoughtfulness, and absorb the richness of its past. When you slow down and open your senses, you'll notice that the spirits of Berlin are everywhere. It's the only town on the Eastern Shore where the spirits have actually been seen walking the streets. Talk to them. Ask them to lead you somewhere special. They'll help you make new discoveries— perhaps a great restaurant or that perfect gift for someone special, a new friend, an insight or an answer to a problem that has been weighing heavily on you. Stop at the healing tree and feel the vibrations of the life force inside it. Lay your troubles and pain at its feet. Experience that mystical quality of America's coolest town.

People are always asking me which ghost walk is my favorite out of the ten I have written. I respond quickly. My favorite is Ocean City. And it's because all the ghosts on the walk (except for one or two) are happy, and the stories are rich and warm. They're about good times and the romance of vacation. The ghosts of Ocean City were so at home when they were alive that they never left. I love the chaotic vibe and the energy of that seaside town. It's hard to match that anywhere.

But if you love ghost walks with historic streetscapes, Berlin is classic. And what Ocean City lacks Berlin pours forth with historical buildings, mystical energy and a quiet small-town feel. They are perfect complements to each other.

Every location in this book was chosen with a reader in mind who loves the seaside and the romance of travel and vacations. Whether you are a native, a visitor or someone who will be able to travel to Ocean City and Berlin only vicariously by reading these stories, my hope is that these sites will come alive in your imagination and enchant you, inspire you to always look deeper and see what lies beneath the surface of every seaside town. Spirits tend to return to where they're happiest, so vacation spots and cool towns will always have more than their fair share.

Most of the places mentioned in this book are open to the public, and those that are not are at least easily viewed from the street. With the exception of the Rackliffe House and Captain's Hill, the sites are on a walkable trail. In an hour or two, you can walk through either town with this book in hand and take yourself on a ghost walk—if you're willing to venture out into haunted territory alone, that is. If you get scared, just talk to the local folks. They'll assure you that you are safe and will offer their own insights to make your experience richer.

May the spirits of Ocean City and Berlin meet you when you arrive, guide you while you're there and bless you when you leave.

BIBLIOGRAPHY

BOOKS

Barth, John. *Lost in the Fun House*. New York: Anchor Books, 1988.

Chappell, Helen. *The Chesapeake Book of the Dead*. Baltimore, MD: Johns Hopkins University Press, 1999.

Corddry, Mary. *City on the Sand: Ocean City, Maryland, and the People Who Built It*. Centreville, MD: Tidewater Publishers, 1991.

Hurley, George, and Suzanne Hurley. *Ocean City Maryland, a Pictorial History*. Virginia Beach, VA: Donning Company Publishers, 1979.

———. *Shipwrecks and Rescues: Along the Barrier Islands of Delaware, Maryland, and Virginia*. Virginia Beach, VA: Donning Company Publishers, 1984.

Katz, Gordon E. *102 Gentlemen & A Lady*. Marceline, MO: Walsworth Publishing Company, 2012.

Matthews, Katie Gaskins, and William Russell. *Worcester County: A Pictorial History*. Virginia Beach, VA: Donning Company Publishers, 1985.

Morgan, Michael. *Ocean City: Going Down the Ocean*. Charleston, SC: The History Press, 2011.

Odd-Fellowship Illustrated: The Complete Revised Ritual of the AJJD the Rebekah Degrees. Chicago, IL: Ezra A. Cook, Publisher, 1893.

Paterson, Jacqueline Memory. *Tree Wisdom*. San Francisco, CA: Thorsons, 1996.

Patton, Tom. *Listen to the Voices, Follow the Trails: Discovering Maryland's Seaside Heritage*. Plainfield, IN: Penned, Ink LLC, 2005.

Prince, E.D. *Delaware and the Eastern Shore of Maryland and Virginia*. Wilmington, DE: John E. Harlan and the Star Publishing Company, 1926.

Schlosser, S.E. *Spooky Maryland: Tales of Hauntings, Strange Happenings, and Other Local Lore.* Guilford, CT: Morris Book Publishing Company, 2007.

Sullivan, C. John. *Old Ocean City: The Journal and Photographs of Robert Craighead Walker, 1904–1916.* Baltimore, MD: Johns Hopkins University Press, 2001.

Taylor, Susan. *Berlin: Images of America.* Charleston, SC: Arcadia Publishing, 2007.

Touart, Paul B. *Along the Seaboard Side.* Snow Hill, MD: Worcester County Commissioners, 1994.

Truit, Dr. Reginald V., and Dr. Millard G. Les Callette. *Worcester County, Maryland's Arcadia.* Snow Hill, MD: Worcester County Historical Society, 1977.

Yon, Michael Phillip. *Danger Close.* Rockwall, TX: Apple Pie Publishing, 2000.

ARTICLES AND PAMPHLETS

Charles, Joan D. "Footnotes to a Legend." Ocean City Life-Saving Station Museum, 1991.

Davis, Arthur T. "Memories of Life on a Sandbar, the Tarry-A-While Guest House." Ocean City Life-Saving Station Museum, 2006.

Delmarva Star. "'Zippy' Lewis' Treasure Haunts Memory of Ocean City Folk." April 22, 1928.

Ferron, Karl Merton. "Randy Hofman, Sculpting a Beach Ministry." *Baltimore Sun*, May 24, 2013.

Folklore Collection Files. "Tarry-A-While" and "The Henry Colored Hotel." Edward H. Nabb Research Center at Salisbury University, 1975.

Guy, Chris. "Summers Apart: The Old Henry's Colored Hotel in Ocean City, Recognized as a Landmark, Might Be Revived as a B&B and Museum." *Baltimore Sun*, 2007.

Harrison, Sandra. "A History of Worcester County, Maryland." Mayor and Council of Berlin, 1958.

Hurley, Suzanne B. "Captain William Carhart." Ocean City Life-Saving Station Museum, 1991.

———. "The Mystique of Zippy Lewis." Ocean City Life-Saving Station Museum, n.d.

Jester, Irma J. "Sal, the Laughing Lady, Queen of the Funhouse." Ocean City Life-Saving Station Museum, 1982.

Katz, Gordon. "Coffin's Bazaar." Ocean City Life-Saving Station Museum Collection, May 2013.

Means, Dennis R. "A Heavy Sea Running: The Formation of the U.S. Life-Saving Service, 1846–1878." *Prologue Magazine* (1987).
Mumford, Dot. "O.C.B.C: Ocean City Before Condominiums." 1989.
"Rosalie Tilghman Shreve." Ocean City Life-Saving Station Museum, n.d.
Scuttlebutt. Ocean City Life-Saving Station Museum, December 15, 2012.
Sheppeck, Mary Ellen Mumford. "A History of Ocean City, Maryland." Mayor and Council of Berlin, 1958.
"Walking Tour of Historic Downtown Ocean City, Maryland." Map. Downtown Association of Ocean City and Ocean City Development Corporation, 2005.
Willis, Dail. "Antique Carousel Prospers at Trimper Park—Wooden Wonder." *Baltimore Sun,* July 17, 1994.

MULTIMEDIA

Once Upon a Sand Dune. Ocean City, MD: Select Media, Inc., for Ocean City Museum Society, 1997/2006.

PERSONAL INTERVIEWS

Kirk Burbage, Burbage Funeral Homes, Berlin, MD
Anna Dolle Bushnell, Dolle's Candy, Ocean City, MD
Cheryl Holland, Calvin B. Taylor House Museum, Berlin, MD
George and Suzanne Hurley, Ocean City, MD
Sandy Hurley, Ocean City Life-Saving Station Museum
Glenn Irwin, Ocean City Development Corporation, Ocean City, MD
Betty Jester, Ocean City, MD
Johnny Jett, Trimper Rides and Amusements, Ocean City, MD
Kyle Johnson and Marge Steele, Dunes Manor Hotel, Ocean City, MD
Missy Mason, Delmarva Spirit Hunters
Denise Milko, Ocean City, MD
Joseph Moore, attorney, Ocean City, MD
Charlie Purnell, Atlantic Hotel, Ocean City, MD
Angela Reynolds, Atlantic Hotel, Berlin, MD
Greg Shockley, Shoreham Hotel, Ocean City, MD
Staff at Adkins Hardware, Berlin, MD
Staff at the Atlantic Hotel, Berlin, MD

BIBLIOGRAPHY

Staff at the Atlantic Hotel, Ocean City, MD
Staff at the Rackliffe Plantation House, Berlin, MD
Staff at Trimper Rides and Amusements, Ocean City, MD
Susan Taylor, Calvin B. Taylor House Museum, Berlin, MD
Robin Tomaselli, Baked Desserts, Berlin, MD
Brooks Trimper, Trimper Rides and Amusements, Ocean City, MD
Jo Ellen West, Ocean City, MD

ABOUT THE AUTHOR

Mindie Burgoyne became interested in ghost stories when she and her husband, Dan, moved into a haunted house in Somerset County, Maryland, in 2002. She began collecting ghost stories about the haunted Eastern Shore and eventually wrote *Haunted Eastern Shore: Ghostly Tales from East of the Chesapeake*, a book published by The History Press in 2009. Her readers began inquiring about ghost tours to some of the places in her book. So she organized a few bus tours and continued to collect ghost stories. In the course of five years, she has collected over 130 ghost stories and designed ten ghost walks in towns across the Delmarva Peninsula. In 2014, she and her husband founded Chesapeake Ghost Walks. They hired and trained ghost tour guides and started a campaign to market a ghost walk trail that runs from Easton to Ocean City. She continues to uncover ghost stories that she publishes on her blogs and in local print publications.

Chesapeake Ghost Walks is a subsidiary of Travel Hag Tours, the Burgoynes' travel company. Under this brand, they offer custom tours designed for those who want a travel experience that feeds the mind, body and spirit. They offer tours every year to Ireland's mystical places and sponsor a travel club for girlfriends in the United States.

About the Author

By day, Mindie works full time for the State of Maryland doing rural economic development, assisting Eastern Shore businesses and local governments by connecting them with resources that will help grow the economy. Additionally, she is on the board of directors for the Edward H. Nabb Research Center at Salisbury University.

Mindie and Dan Burgoyne have six children and ten grandchildren. They love the outdoors and spend most of their free time traveling. She writes from their home in Marion Station, Maryland.

Visit us at
www.historypress.net
....
This title is also available as an e-book